VEGAN PASTRY

VEGAN PASTRY

PIERRE HERMÉ
with Linda Vongdara

GRUB STREET · LONDON

Published in 2024 by
Grub Street
4 Rainham Close
London
SW11 6SS

Email: food@grubstreet.co.uk
Web: www.grubstreet.co.uk
Twitter: @grub_street
Facebook: Grub Street Publishing
Instagram: grubstreetpublishinguk

Copyright this English language edition © Grub Street 2024
ISBN 978-1-911714-16-3
A CIP catalogue for this book is available from the British Library

Published originally in French as Pâtisserie Végétale
Copyright © 2023 Éditions Solar, un département d'Edi8, Paris

Photography: Laurent Fau
Styling: Sarah Vasseghi

All rights reserved. No part of this publication may be reproduced, stored in a retrieval system or transmitted in any form or by any means electronic, mechanical, photocopying, recording or otherwise without the prior permission of the publisher

Printed and bound by Finidr, Czechia

Contents

Foreward	6
Introduction	8
Key points for successful vegan pastry	11

Viennoiseries

To eat with your fingers — 16

Travel cakes

An invitation to escape — 44

Chocolate desserts and bonbons

Chocolate addict — 80

Fruit desserts and tarts

Fruity and sweet — 118

Ice creams and sorbets

Frosted delights — 162

Macarons

A couple of grams of happiness — 178

Plated desserts

Desserts to share...or not — 202

Index by ingredients	248
Recipes index	254
Acknowledgements	256

Foreword

In recent years, pastry-making has undergone a major change. In the 1960s, Gaston Lenôtre pioneered a different kind of pâtisserie based on extensive research and constantly renewed creativity. However today it's social media and the power of images that have elevated our sweet creations to an art form. But beyond the visual, our job is above all about taste! The taste of good butter in viennoiseries, of milk, cream and eggs in an excellent cake.

Vegan pastry-making, meanwhile, is developing discreetly in France, in response to a gradually increasing demand, but all too often it remains in the realms of curiosity and approximation. Perhaps this is because it's not visually appetising, or because its taste isn't what we're used to. I didn't get interested in vegan cuisine until later on, as the no-animal-ingredients approach wasn't representative of my daily life. My current interest in this approach was sparked by discovering the cuisine of Jean-Georges Vongerichten in New York at his ABCV restaurant in 2018, and then the pastries of Rodolphe Landemaine when he opened his Land&Monkeys bakery in Paris. Far from my preconceptions, this cuisine and these desserts, both delicate and tasty, have opened up a whole new world of possibilities for me. I set myself to vegan pastry-making with the same rigour and professionalism as I do with traditional pastry-making. I was given the opportunity to do this when I started working with La Maison du Chocolat in 2020. I had to come up with two new chocolate pastries and think about how I could add to the excellence of this boutique. Vegan pastry was an obvious choice. It allowed me to offer a different type of pastry, following on from the 'Wellbeing' chocolate boxes presented some time previously by Nicolas Cloiseau. I had the idea and the motivation, I just had to put them into practice by imagining a new gourmet language. I developed the Rose des Sables and Fleur de Cassis desserts as a way of getting my foot in the door, imagining the future and perhaps forcing fate. But making two vegan pastries wasn't enough to capture the richness of this new world.

In the world of creation, you should never be afraid of confronting the unknown; you have to take risks. Setting myself the goal of writing a book about this different approach is part of this quest. It's a challenge to be taken up, an obligation to break free from tradition, to deepen my knowledge and get out of my comfort zone. It allows us to embark on an extensive quest for tastiness and to propose a new story of pastries and emotions. But to take on a new discipline in a fair and relevant way the first step is to learn. You can't become a vegan pastry chef overnight. You have to acquire an in-depth knowledge of the ingredients, understand how to use them and develop a new way of thinking to create delicious recipes. In short, you have to unlearn the basics and open up to alternatives. There are currently no tables or pre-established rules giving you the equivalent substitutes for eggs, butter or cream. It's all a question of combining elements to find the right compromise and make a successful gateau. This empirical approach has involved a number of more or less successful attempts. My meeting with Linda Vongdara and the work of my team in the creative workshop (R&D) have enabled me to grasp this new knowledge.

This book is based on my philosophy, with pleasure as its only guide. I'm not trying to discover the taste of butter, eggs or cream, I simply want to offer you a new creative opportunity, a new way of tasting. The aim here is not to reproduce the texture of a traditional pastry, but to open up to another point of view, other flavours, other sensations and other ways of doing things. Fascinatingly vegan, different, just as good and sometimes even better than traditional pâtisserie: I even surprised myself when I tasted the infinitely delicious creations with their evanescent textures and flavours. Changing perspective to evolve is part of my philosophy.

This new opus is an invitation to explore difference by discovering my vegan interpretation of some of our great classics, as well as new creations and recipes from my co-author Linda Vongdara.

Pierre Hermé

Introduction

Vegan pastry, like conventional pastry, has a duty to provide indulgence and emotion. This gastronomically Oulipian exercise in style was born out of the need to change our eating habits in the interests of ecology and animal welfare. This new practice, which will undoubtedly become a discipline and know-how in its own right, is overturning centuries of culinary tradition. It's about questioning our heritage and rethinking recipes without the fundamental ingredients that have shaped French pastry-making throughout its history.

After training in traditional pastry-making, I realised that there was a lack of knowledge in vegan practices. So I set out to create some tricks of the trade and recipes, a methodology that would enable me to make perfect pastries à *la française*. I was keen to contribute to the development of a new knowledge through a complete repertoire and to propose an effective matrix for creating sweet products in line with our world and its new challenges.

If you have to replace eggs in vegan baking, don't be fooled into thinking that there are easy substitutes like apple compote or chia seeds. This type of solution, which is very popular on social networks, conveys a simplistic image of vegan pastry-making. In fact, a direct replacement would result in a pâtisserie that is less pleasant and less tasty. And that's definitely not the type of pastry we're aiming for. This time we won't be racking the brains of Antonin Carême and Jules Gouffé, the founding fathers of French pastry-making. As a good student, I went back to my pastry technology classes, and it was as an explorer, accompanied by teachers, chefs, pastry chefs, bakers, researchers and engineers, that I began an experiment that lasted around six years and which enabled me to share this emerging know-how at my school, L'Okara. Like martial arts, each school has its own style and founding principles. I wanted to create methods, recipes and bases with unique names – such as moffa, leonard biscuit, alba cream, estérelle and fomico mousse – to highlight a discipline with its own identity.

I believe in the 'good taste of simplicity' as described by Auguste Escoffier and also agree with him when he writes, 'Simplicity does not exclude beauty'. My work is always accompanied by a desire to refine the recipes to bring out the full flavour of the raw ingredients. It's important to me to respect this precious plant material, which comes from the earth and is then transformed by our hands as artisans. For this rather complex vegan pastry, I opted for simplicity.

It was with this in mind that I approached the man who, for me, is the best pastry chef in the world and whose international renown and talent are well established: Pierre Hermé.

To help pastry-making evolve in a significant way, I needed a talented artist, an iconic figure who would get on board with me. That's the story behind this book.

Linda Vongdara

Key points for successful vegan pastry

It's difficult to talk about vegan pastry without a series of certain bases and uses. This introduction features a few key points to be aware of before taking the plunge. In my opinion, three elements are essential: the starches, emulsions and baking. Sugars and taste are also covered.

STARCHES
Foundation and structure

Flours, with or without gluten, are amylaceous products, i.e. they contain starch. The starch and gluten contained in flours are the main natural structuring agents in both traditional and vegan pastry-making, as they thicken creams and solidify cakes by gelling. Their effects can be optimised by hydrating the flours and/or starches first, followed by a rest period of at least 20 minutes to allow the starches to develop texture. Although this may seem surprising, the mere presence of these two elements already largely replaces eggs and their coagulation action.

Some starches (rice flour, maize starch, potato starch) are also relatively stable in humidity, when frozen and when conserved. With a little time and know-how, these natural starches can be used to make all kinds of vegan pastry creations, even the most technical ones. But for greater speed, efficiency and sometimes stability, you can choose to accelerate the process by using texturisers such as xanthan gum, guar gum or pectin.

For gluten-free products, the viscous action of gluten has to be replaced by adding thickeners (flaxseed, chia seeds or psyllium, for example). This helps to maintain sufficient viscoelasticity to allow the dough to swell flexibly and maintain the hold and softness of a brioche, biscuit or cake after baking. These thickeners play a role in the texture of the cakes.

EMULSIONS
Fats, taste and texture

Fats are necessary to develop flavours, while also contributing to texture. If you opt for a liquid oil, your creams will be more fluid and cakes softer. With a fat that solidifies at room temperature, such as cocoa butter or coconut oil, the creams will hold better. There's also the notion of fondant cake textures and the possibility of whipping creams to aerate them. Among solid fats, deodorised coconut oil can be used to add hold and a fondant texture to creations while remaining neutral in taste. A small amount of cocoa butter is used to give texture to cream or to whip emulsions. This is the case for estérelle cream, inspired by the process of making whipped ganache. Generally speaking, solid fats have the ability to expand a cream and contribute to the final texture by solidifying as they set again when cold.

The melting temperature of these fats also plays an important role in the perception and pleasant sensations experienced during tasting. Here are a few examples: alba cream is a whipped cream made from deodorised coconut oil, which quickly goes from a solid to a liquid state, with a melting point of between 20°C and 25°C. This cream melts quickly in the mouth, leaving an impression of little fat and lightness. Estérelle cream, the equivalent of classic chantilly cream, is made from cocoa butter that melts at around 37°C. The result is a longer-lasting flavour with a richer, fatter texture. So, depending on the fat used, the result will be different.

As far as vegetable fats are concerned, all oils, whether liquid or solid at room temperature, can be used in vegan pastry. Non-deodorised coconut oil or olive oil, for example, are interesting due to their taste. Liquid oils such as grapeseed oil, peanut oil or sunflower oil add smoothness to the final result and have the advantage of being neutral in taste.

It is very important to note that fats must be emulsified in the preparations, as the emulsion — i.e. the stable mixture of water and fats — plays a role in the perception of taste and in the final structure of the pastry. This is crucial to the success of vegan pastries.

In traditional pastry-making, the presence of eggs and dairy products alone guarantees a beautiful emulsion thanks to the surfactants they naturally contain. However, when making vegan pastries, you need to use ingredients containing natural emulsifying agents, such as soya-based products (containing lecithin) or chickpeas (as flour). Other natural ingredients such as lupin and flaxseed are also emulsifiers. It is also possible to obtain emulsifying products such as sunflower lecithin or emulsifying vegetable fibres, such as citrus fibre used in ice creams and flax fibre, to give a stable texture to creations. Note that thickeners and gelling agents will help stabilise an emulsion.

Margarines are best for puff pastry and other pastries. They have the plasticity of butter and make kneading easier, unlike cocoa butter, which is preferred for making brioches that do not require kneading. Margarines also have the advantage of making biscuits soft and supple, while being neutral in flavour.

BAKING
Solidification

The final key point is how to bake vegan pastries. There are a few simple rules to follow: bake cake mixes for longer, at higher temperatures (as when baking bread), and leave them to cool so that the structure sets. Note that the structuring action of solidification will not occur at the same time depending on whether you are making a gateau with eggs, a vegan gateau with wheat flour, or a gluten-free vegan gateau.

SUGARS
Their role in pastry

In traditional pastry the choice of sugars influences texture, taste and conservation. These properties are the same for vegan pastry. But here, the trick is to dissolve the sugar in the vegan milk before adding it to the flours to optimise their hydration.

AND WHAT ABOUT TASTE?
Flavouring agents and enhancers

Deprived of the taste of eggs and butter, fruit and chocolate flavours often become more intense. On the other hand, for the pastries and brioches, the absence of butter diminishes their taste; nevertheless, the very crisp textures of the pastries and the airy texture of the brioches make these creations delicious.

COOKING SETTINGS FOR VEGAN PASTRIES

CAKE SHAPE	TYPE OF PASTRY	TEMPERATURE SETTING	FAN SETTINGS	COOKING TIME
Large gateaux, baked in deep tins and high rings	Cakes to share Layered gateaux Large travel cakes	160°C–180°C	No fan or low fan	30 minutes for a 6-portion cake to 2 hours for a very large cake (more than 30 portions)
Flat gateaux baked in flared tins	Chocolate gateaux Brownies Walnut gateaux Flat travel cakes High-fat pastries	180°C–200°C	Low fan (for chocolate pastries) to medium fan (for other pastries)	15–20 minutes
Thin gateaux baked on a tray	Leonard biscuit Dessert sponges Sponge for rolls	200°C	Medium to high fan	10 minutes
Small individual gateaux	Mini-cakes Financiers Madeleines Individual petit-fours	Start cooking at 220°C–240°C. Continue at 180°C if necessary depending on size	Medium to high fan	2–5 minutes at the high temperature to start, then 5–8 minutes at the lower temperature
Biscuits and shortbread	Biscuits Sweet shortcrust pastry Pastry shell	150°C–170°C	No fan or low fan	15–30 minutes, depending on temperature, until evenly coloured
Filled tarts	Apple tarts Fruit tarts	180°C–190°C	Low or medium fan	30–45 minutes depending on fruit and toppings

Key points for successful vegan pastry

Viennoiseries

To eat with your fingers

Synonymous with butter, fresh eggs and crisp, golden puff pastry, viennoiseries have always been an insatiable indulgence for me. But what happens to the taste and texture so emblematic of our country when its main ingredient, butter, disappears from the recipe?

The vegan approach to viennoiseries is a new opportunity to bring an unexpected lightness and freshness to the textures. While comparisons with traditional versions are hard to avoid, this is not the approach. When fine-tuning the recipes, I only let myself be guided by the sensations and the pleasure I experienced when tasting.

During this work, we had to familiarise ourselves with vegetable oils, cocoa butter, lecithin and mixed seeds, such as chia and flaxseed. While the turning and baking techniques are the same as for butter viennoiseries, the list of ingredients is longer and more complex. You need to make the effort to find high-quality natural ingredients, then learn how to allocate their roles, combine them and incorporate them at the right temperature and in a precise order.

I had to get off the beaten track and experiment with other recipes to achieve the pleasure of a viennoiserie just out of the oven, golden, crisp and soft. But creativity has no bounds; developing these bakery creations was a new challenge. When we made the first brioche recipe, I didn't know what to expect. And I have to admit that I was surprised and bewildered by the result. For the first time I was discovering the evanescent, light, soft texture of a vegan brioche. It was an almost surreal tasting experience. The experience was similar when I tasted the first croissant. I was brought up with a taste for margarine. In the 1950s, my father used it to work all his doughs, except for kouglof, for which he used butter. With the vegan pastries, I rediscovered that special taste, a familiar childhood flavour, even if butter is still my favourite... The crispness of these butter-free croissants gripped me and made me forget the absence of this wonderful fat. As for the toppings, they play a major part in the taste and enjoyment.

Of course, for each of these creations, there's no need to try and recreate the taste of traditional viennoiseries. The experience is quite different, and is approached with a focus on pleasure and indulgence.

Brioche

One of the first recipes we made was the brioche, which left a lasting impression on me. The combination of hydrated seeds and vegetable fats gives it an incredibly light texture, which makes you forget that there's no butter. It also maintains the delightful softness of the brioche.

Pierre Hermé

Makes 3 brioches

Preparation time: 3 hours
Resting time: 17-18 hours
Cooking time: 40 minutes

FOR THE HYDRATED SEED MIX (PREPARE THE DAY BEFORE)
10 g chia seeds
10 g flaxseed
10 g rolled oats
30 g still mineral water

Using a food processor, coarsely blend the seeds and oats 30 minutes before preparing the brioche dough, to allow the seeds to hydrate. Add the water at room temperature.

VIENNOISERIES *To eat with your fingers*

FOR THE BRIOCHE DOUGH
(PREPARE THE DAY BEFORE)
107.5 g cocoa butter (Valrhona®)
107.5 g deodorised coconut oil
425 g T45 flour
65 g caster sugar
20 g fresh yeast
6 g sunflower lecithin
310 g still mineral water
10 g Guérande fleur de sel
60 g hydrated seed mix

Melt the deodorised coconut oil and cocoa butter, then keep the mixture at 25°C. Place the sifted flour, sugar, fresh yeast and sunflower lecithin in the bowl of a food processor fitted with a dough hook or a flat beater attachment for small quantities. Run the processor on speed 1 and add around 70% of the still mineral water. Let the dough rise on speed 1 and add the remaining water in two batches, allowing it to rise between each addition. As soon as the dough comes away from the sides of the bowl, add the fleur de sel, the hydrated seeds and the mixture of cocoa butter and deodorised coconut oil melted at 25°C. Run the processor on speed 2 and wait for the dough to come away from the sides of the bowl. Transfer to a mixing bowl, cover with cling film in direct contact and leave to rise for 1 hour at room temperature. Fold the dough over slightly and set aside in the fridge to rise for 2 hours to 2 hours 30 minutes. Fold the dough over again and set aside in the fridge for about 12 hours. As soon as the dough is uniformly cold it is ready to be worked and rolled out to make brioche mousseline, brioche Nanterre or a brioche loaf.

VARIATIONS
BRIOCHE MOUSSELINE
Brioche dough
Margarine (as needed)

Collect 3 850-ml tin cans (99 mm x 118 mm) 10 cm in diameter and 12 cm high. Remove the paper label, wash them in clean water, dry them and grease them with margarine, then 'bake' them in a fan oven at 250°C for 7-8 minutes. As soon as they are out of the oven, wipe them with a clean cloth. The moulds are ready for use. Lightly grease the base with margarine. Line the inside of the moulds with greaseproof paper measuring 30 x 35 cm. Shape the brioche dough into balls weighing around 350 g by folding the corners into the centre and rolling between your hands. Place each ball of pastry in a mould and, using a rolling pin, lightly smooth the pastry on the base of the mould. Leave to rest in a room at 28°C for 3-4 hours, until the pastry extends 1-2 cm over the edges of the moulds. Bake the brioches in a fan oven at 170°C for around 40 minutes, opening the oven door for a few seconds every 10 minutes to let the moisture escape. Allow to cool before turning out.

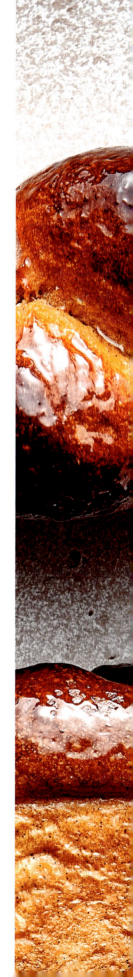

BRIOCHE NANTERRE
Brioche dough
Margarine (as needed)

Lightly grease 4 tin cake moulds measuring 14 x 8 cm and 8 cm high. Divide the dough into 12 85-g pieces. Shape them into balls and place 3 of them side by side in each mould, pressing lightly. Leave to stand in a room at 28°C for 2 hours. Bake the brioches in a fan oven at 160°C for around 45 minutes, opening the oven door for a few seconds every 10 minutes to let the moisture escape. Allow to cool before turning out.

BRIOCHE LOAF
950 g brioche dough
Margarine (as needed)

Lightly grease a 50 x 8 cm and 8 cm high cake tin with straight sides. Shape the dough into a ball and press lightly into the tin. Leave to stand in a room at 28°C for 3 hours. Bake the brioche in a fan oven at 160°C for around 45-55 minutes, opening the oven door for a few seconds every 10 minutes to let the moisture escape. Allow to cool before turning out.

Rolled cinnamon brioche

Delicious for breakfast or as an afternoon snack, the rolled cinnamon brioche is perfect for sharing. Very soft, the sections can be teased apart easily by hand.

Linda Vongdara

Makes 2 brioches for 6-7 people

Preparation time: 3 hours
Resting time: 17 hours
Cooking time: 40 minutes

FOR THE HYDRATED SEED MIX (PREPARE THE DAY BEFORE)
10 g chia seeds
10 g flaxseed
10 g rolled oats
30 g still mineral water

Using a food processor, coarsely blend the seeds and oats 30 minutes before preparing the brioche dough, to allow the seeds to hydrate. Add the water at room temperature.

FOR THE BRIOCHE DOUGH (PREPARE THE DAY BEFORE)

107.5 g cocoa butter (Valrhona®)
107.5 g deodorised coconut oil
425 g T45 flour
65 g caster sugar
20 g fresh yeast
6 g sunflower lecithin
310 g still mineral water
10 g Guérande fleur de sel
60 g hydrated seed mix

Melt the deodorised coconut oil and cocoa butter, then keep the mixture at 25°C. Place the sifted flour, sugar, fresh yeast and sunflower lecithin in the bowl of a food processor fitted with a dough hook or a flat beater attachment for small quantities. Run the processor on speed 1 and add around 70% of the still mineral water. Let the dough thicken on speed 1 and add the remaining water in two stages, letting the dough thicken between each addition. As soon as the dough comes away from the sides of the bowl, add the fleur de sel, the hydrated seeds and the mixture of cocoa butter and deodorised coconut oil melted at 25°C. Run the processor on speed 2 and wait for the dough to come away from the sides of the bowl. Transfer to a mixing bowl, cover with cling film in direct contact and leave to rise for 1 hour at room temperature. Fold the dough over slightly and set aside in the fridge to rise for 2 hours to 2 hours 30 minutes. Fold the dough over again and set aside in the fridge for about 12 hours. As soon as the dough is uniformly cold it is ready to be worked and rolled out.

FOR THE ROLLED CINNAMON BRIOCHE

880 g brioche dough
50 g margarine
60 g brown sugar
10 g ground cinnamon
A little soya or oat milk

In the bowl of a food processor fitted with a flat beater attachment, process the margarine until softened. Add the sugar and cinnamon and process until the mixture has a creamy texture. Lightly grease a pastry ring 16 cm in diameter and 6 cm high and place it on a baking tray lined with greaseproof paper. Divide the dough into 2 pieces. Roll out each piece of dough on a lightly floured work surface into a rectangle measuring 35 x 25 cm and 7-8 mm thick. Using an offset spatula, spread the margarine/cinnamon/sugar mixture very thinly over the brioche dough. Roll up the brioche lengthways. Using a sharp knife, cut the resulting roll into 7 even pieces. Arrange 6 rolls vertically around the edges of the ring, then place one in the middle. Brush the surface with a little soya or oat milk. Leave to rise for 2 hours at 28°C.

FOR THE CRUMBLE

50 g T65 wheat flour or brown rice flour
50 g light brown sugar
40 g cold margarine
2 g Guérande fleur de sel

Using your fingertips, coarsely mix all the ingredients in a mixing bowl to obtain a crumbly mixture. Set aside in the fridge until ready to use.

COOKING AND FINISHING

Preheat the fan oven to 170°C. Cover the tops of the brioches with the crumble. Bake for about 40 minutes. Allow to cool slightly before turning out.

Babka

Babka, a brioche of Polish origin, has become a classic among bakers in recent years. I like to top this very light version with a homemade chocolate spread rich with hazelnuts.

Linda Vongdara

Makes 2 brioches for 6 people

Preparation time: 3 hours
Resting time: 15 hours
Cooking time: 40 minutes

FOR THE HYDRATED SEED MIX (PREPARE THE DAY BEFORE)

10 g chia seeds
10 g flaxseed
10 g rolled oats
30 g still mineral water

Using a food processor, coarsely blend the seeds and oats 30 minutes before preparing the brioche dough, to allow the seeds to hydrate. Add the water at room temperature.

FOR THE BRIOCHE DOUGH (PREPARE THE DAY BEFORE)

107.5 g cocoa butter (Valrhona®)
107.5 g deodorised coconut oil
425 g T45 flour
65 g caster sugar
20 g fresh yeast
6 g sunflower lecithin
310 g still mineral water
10 g Guérande fleur de sel
60 g hydrated seed mix

Melt the deodorised coconut oil and cocoa butter, then keep the mixture at 25°C. Place the sifted flour, sugar, fresh yeast and sunflower lecithin in the bowl of a food processor fitted with a dough hook or a flat beater attachment for small quantities. Run the processor on speed 1 and add around 70% of the still mineral water. Let the dough thicken on speed 1 and add the remaining water in two stages, letting the dough thicken between each addition. As soon as the dough comes away from the sides of the bowl, add the fleur de sel, the hydrated seeds and the mixture of cocoa butter and deodorised coconut oil melted at 25°C. Run the processor on speed 2 and wait for the dough to come away from the sides of the bowl. Transfer to a mixing bowl, cover with cling film in direct contact and leave to rise for 1 hour at room temperature. Fold the dough over slightly and set aside in the fridge to rise for 2 hours to 2 hours 30 minutes. Fold the dough over again and set aside in the fridge for about 12 hours. As soon as the dough is uniformly cold it is ready to be worked and rolled out.

FOR THE FINISHING
880 g brioche dough
380 g chocolate spread
200 g neutral glaze diluted with 50% still mineral water

SHAPING, COOKING AND FINISHING

Lightly grease 2 pastry rings 16 cm in diameter and place on baking trays lined with greaseproof paper. Divide the brioche dough into 2 pieces. Roll out each dough piece on a lightly floured work surface into a rectangle measuring 35 x 25 cm and 7-8 mm thick. Using an offset spatula, add a thin layer of chocolate spread over the brioche dough. Roll up the brioche lengthways. Using a sharp, lightly greased knife, cut the roll in half along its length in the centre. Twist the two parts together, taking care to place the cut-out part with the spread on top, then roll the twist over itself, like a snail. Carefully place the babkas in the centre of the rings. Leave to rise for 2 hours at 28°C. Preheat the fan oven to 170°C. Bake the babkas for around 40 minutes. Then glaze them while they are still warm with a little diluted neutral glaze. Allow to cool before turning out.

Croissant

For our classic croissants, we work with a fairly high salt/sugar balance, which is one of their distinctive features. In the vegan version, this balance is preserved and the crispness is so impressive that it overrides the intrinsic, fairly neutral taste of the croissant. I let myself be carried away by these sensations.

Pierre Hermé

Makes 10 croissants

Preparation time: 4 hours
Resting time: 20 hours
Cooking time: 20-25 minutes

FOR THE CROISSANT DOUGH (PREPARE THE DAY BEFORE)
8 g Guérande fleur de sel
95 g still mineral water
66 g oat milk
340 g T45 fine wheat flour
25 g margarine
50 g caster sugar
8 g fresh yeast

In a mixing bowl, dissolve the fleur de sel in the water and the oat milk using a whisk.

In the bowl of a food processor fitted with a dough hook, add the previous mixture (fleur de sel/water/oat milk), then add all the other ingredients and mix the dough for 5 minutes on speed 1, then 17-20 minutes on speed 2. At the end of kneading, the dough should be at 24-25°C.

1) As soon as you have finished kneading, shape the dough into a tight ball. Cover with cling film and place in a room at 25°C for 1 hour.
2) Place the dough in the fridge for 4 hours, then roll out into a 10 cm square.
3) Rewrap the dough in cling film and refrigerate overnight.

FOR THE CROISSANT DOUGH PREPARATION

Croissant dough (the recipe above)
215 g unsalted margarine,
  at room temperature, 18-19°C

Remove the croissant dough from the fridge. Pound the margarine with a rolling pin to make it smooth and square. On a lightly floured work surface, roll out the dough into a square about twice the size of the margarine.

ENCASING AND TURNING

Place the square of margarine in the middle of the dough square and close so that you can no longer see the margarine. Once the margarine is encased, make two simple turns, then place the dough in the fridge for 45 minutes before the third and final simple turn.

Place the dough in the freezer for 1 hour before rolling it out.

ROLLING OUT, DETAILING AND SHAPING

On a lightly floured work surface, roll out the dough to a thickness of about 3 mm and a length of 30 cm. Loosen the dough and cut into regular triangles, with 9 cm width, weighing around 85 g. Roll up the croissants, not too tightly to allow the dough to expand. Seal underneath. Place them on a baking tray lined with greaseproof paper and refrigerate for 2 hours.

FOR THE GLAZE

50 g soya milk
15 g maple syrup

Mix the soya milk and maple syrup in a bowl and refrigerate.

COOKING AND FINISHING

Remove the tray from the fridge and leave the croissants to rise for 2-3 hours in a room at 28°C. Preheat the fan oven to 190°C. Brush the croissants with the glaze, then put them in the oven, lowering the temperature to 170°C and bake for 20-25 minutes, opening the oven door for a few seconds every 8 minutes to let the moisture escape. As soon as they come out of the oven, place on a stainless steel rack.

Ispahan croissant

This recipe has the crispness of a croissant, while the flavour is provided by the trio of rose, raspberry and lychee, whose notes are heightened by the absence of butter.

Pierre Hermé

Makes 10 croissants

Preparation time: 6 hours
Resting time: 18 hours
Cooking time: 40-45 minutes

FOR THE CROISSANT DOUGH (PREPARE THE DAY BEFORE)
8 g Guérande fleur de sel
95 g still mineral water
66 g oat milk
340 g T45 fine wheat flour
25 g margarine
50 g caster sugar
8 g fresh yeast

In a mixing bowl, dissolve the fleur de sel in the water and the oat milk using a whisk.

In the bowl of a food processor fitted with a dough hook, add the previous mixture (fleur de sel/water/oat milk), then add all the other ingredients and mix the dough for 5 minutes on speed 1, then 17-20 minutes on speed 2. At the end of kneading, the dough should be at 24-25°C.

1) As soon as you have finished kneading, shape the dough into a tight ball. Cover with cling film and place in a room at 25°C for 1 hour.
2) Place the dough in the fridge for 4 hours, then roll out into a 10 cm square.
3) Rewrap the dough in cling film and refrigerate overnight.

FOR THE ROSE ALMOND PASTE (PREPARE THE DAY BEFORE)

250 g almond paste (65% almonds)
1.5 g alcoholic rose extract
A few drops of natural red food colouring

In the bowl of a food processor fitted with a flat beater attachment, mix all the ingredients and spread the paste between two sheets of plastic using a rolling pin. Cut out a rectangle measuring approximately 40 x 10 cm and cut 10 triangles measuring 7 cm wide by 12 cm long. Place in the freezer on a sheet of greaseproof paper and wrap in cling film until ready to use.

FOR THE RASPBERRY AND LYCHEE COMPOTE

40 g lychees in syrup
60 g caster sugar
10 g gellan gum
400 g raspberry purée

Drain the lychees. Cut them roughly and drain them as much as possible. Mix the sugar with the gellan gum and the cold purée, then bring to the boil while stirring. Remove from the heat and add the lychees. On a baking tray covered with a silicone mat, place a baking frame measuring approximately 20 x 10 cm and pour in the raspberry and lychee compote. Leave to cool and gel, then cut into 10 sticks measuring 7 x 2 cm. Store in the freezer wrapped in cling film.

FOR THE CROISSANT DOUGH PREPARATION

Croissant dough (the recipe above)
215 g unsalted margarine,
    at room temperature, 18-19°C

Remove the croissant dough from the fridge. Pound the margarine with a rolling pin to make it smooth and square. On a lightly floured work surface, roll out the dough into a square about twice the size of the margarine.

ENCASING AND TURNING

Place the square of margarine in the middle of the dough square and close so that you can no longer see the margarine. Once the margarine is encased, make two simple turns, then place the dough in the fridge for 45 minutes before the third and final simple turn.

Place the dough in the freezer for 1 hour before rolling it out.

ROLLING OUT, DETAILING AND SHAPING

On a lightly floured work surface, roll out the dough to a thickness of about 3 mm and a length of 30 cm. Loosen the dough and cut into regular triangles, with 9 cm width, weighing around 85 g. Place a triangle of almond paste on each triangle of pastry. Roll up the croissants, not too tightly to allow the dough to expand. Seal underneath. Place them on a baking tray lined with greaseproof paper and refrigerate for 2 hours.

FOR THE GLAZE
50 g soya milk
15 g maple syrup

Mix the soya milk and maple syrup in a bowl and refrigerate.

WATER ICING
250 g icing sugar
50 g still mineral water

Mix the icing sugar and water and place the mixture in the fridge.

COOKING AND FINISHING

Remove the tray from the fridge and leave the croissants to rise for 2–3 hours in a room at 28°C. Preheat the fan oven to 190°C. Brush the croissants with the glaze, then put them in the oven, lowering the temperature to 170°C and bake for 20–25 minutes, opening the oven door for a few seconds every 8 minutes to let the moisture escape.

FOR THE FINISHING
Water icing
50 g freeze-dried raspberries

After removing from the oven, let cool slightly. Dip the surface of the croissants in the water icing, place them on a wire rack to drain off any excess glaze and sprinkle with freeze-dried raspberries. Place on a stainless steel rack.

Almond croissants

In the same way as the Ispahan croissant, the taste and indulgence of these croissants are provided by the almond paste, which makes you forget that there is no butter. This paste must be of excellent quality, as the fact there is no animal fat enhances the flavour of the other ingredients.

Pierre Hermé

Makes 10 croissants

Preparation time: 6 hours
Resting time: 18 hours
Cooking time: 30-40 minutes

FOR THE CROISSANT DOUGH (PREPARE THE DAY BEFORE)

8 g Guérande fleur de sel
95 g still mineral water
66 g oat milk
340 g T45 fine wheat flour
25 g margarine
50 g caster sugar
8 g fresh yeast

In a mixing bowl, dissolve the fleur de sel in the water and the oat milk using a whisk.

In the bowl of a food processor fitted with a dough hook, add the previous mixture (fleur de sel/water/oat milk), then add all the other ingredients and mix the dough for 5 minutes on speed 1, then 17-20 minutes on speed 2. At the end of kneading, the dough should be at 24-25°C.

1) As soon as you have finished kneading, shape the dough into a tight ball. Cover with cling film and place in a room at 25°C for 1 hour.
2) Place the dough in the fridge for 4 hours, then roll out into a 10 cm square.
3) Rewrap the dough in cling film and refrigerate overnight.

FOR THE SUGAR SYRUP (1260 DENISTY AT 30°B) (PREPARE THE DAY BEFORE)

70 g caster sugar
65 g still mineral water

Bring the water and sugar to the boil, skim off any impurities, leave to cool and set aside in an airtight container in the fridge.

VIENNOISERIES *To eat with your fingers*

FOR THE MELT-IN-THE-MOUTH ALMOND PASTE WITH WALNUTS AND HAZELNUTS (PREPARE THE DAY BEFORE)

145 g unpeeled walnuts
145 g unpeeled Piedmont hazelnuts
145 g unpeeled whole almonds
370 g caster sugar
115 g 1260 sugar syrup

In the bowl of a food processor, blend the walnuts, hazelnuts, almonds and sugar. Transfer this mixture into the bowl of a food processor fitted with a flat beater attachment, add the syrup and blend on speed 1. Refrigerate overnight before rolling out the paste to a thickness of 10 mm using a rolling pin. Cut into 10 rectangles measuring 1.5 x 4 cm.

FOR THE CROISSANT DOUGH PREPARATION

Croissant dough (the recipe above)
215 g unsalted margarine, at room temperature, 18–19°C

Remove the croissant dough from the fridge. Pound the margarine with a rolling pin to make it smooth and square. On a lightly floured work surface, roll out the dough into a square about twice the size of the margarine.

ENCASING AND TURNING

Place the square of margarine in the middle of the dough square and close so that you can no longer see the margarine.

Once the margarine is encased, make two simple turns, then place the dough in the fridge for 45 minutes before the third and final simple turn.

Place the dough in the freezer for 1 hour before rolling it out.

ROLLING OUT, CUTTING AND SHAPING

On a lightly floured work surface, roll out the dough to a thickness of about 3 mm and a length of 30 cm. Loosen the dough and cut into regular triangles, with 9 cm width, weighing around 85 g. Place a rectangle of almond paste on each triangle of pastry. Roll up the croissants, not too tightly to allow the dough to expand. Seal underneath. Place them on a baking tray lined with greaseproof paper and refrigerate for 2 hours.

FOR THE TOASTED FLAKED ALMONDS
200 g flaked white almonds

Spread the almonds on a baking tray lined with greaseproof paper and bake for 12-15 minutes at 170°C.

FOR THE GLAZE
50 g soya milk
15 g maple syrup

Mix the soya milk and maple syrup in a bowl and refrigerate.

WATER ICING
250 g icing sugar
50 g still mineral water

Mix the icing sugar and water and place the mixture in the fridge.

COOKING AND FINISHING

Remove the tray from the fridge and leave the croissants to rise for 2-3 hours in a room at 28°C. Preheat the fan oven to 190°C. Brush the croissants with the water icing, then put them in the oven, lowering the temperature to 170°C and bake for 20-25 minutes, opening the oven door for a few seconds every 8 minutes to let the moisture escape.

FOR FINISHING
Water icing
100 g toasted flaked almonds

After removing from the oven, let cool slightly. Dip the surface of the croissants in the water icing, place them on a wire rack to drain off any excess glaze and sprinkle with toasted flaked almonds. Place on a stainless steel rack.

Pain au chocolat with pistachio

In the pain au chocolat, our homemade filling is a mixture of chocolate and gianduja. Here, the homemade chocolate batons combine with the flavour of the pistachio almond paste and the light, crisp texture of the puff pastry to make a sumptuous pastry.

Pierre Hermé

Makes 10 pains au chocolat

Preparation time: 6 hours
Resting time: 18 hours
Cooking time: 35-40 minutes

FOR THE CROISSANT DOUGH (PREPARE THE DAY BEFORE)
8 g Guérande fleur de sel
95 g still mineral water
66 g oat milk
340 g T45 fine wheat flour
25 g margarine
50 g caster sugar
8 g fresh yeast

In a mixing bowl, dissolve the fleur de sel in the water and the oat milk using a whisk.

In the bowl of a food processor fitted with a dough hook, add the previous mixture (fleur de sel/water/oat milk), then add all the other ingredients and mix the dough for 5 minutes on speed 1, then 17-20 minutes on speed 2. At the end of kneading, the dough should be at 24-25°C.

1) As soon as you have finished kneading, shape the dough into a tight ball. Cover with cling film and place in a room at 25°C for 1 hour.
2) Place the dough in the fridge for 4 hours, then roll out into a 10 cm square.
3) Rewrap the dough in cling film and refrigerate overnight.

FOR THE CHOCOLATE BATONS
200 g dark chocolate (Mexico 64% Valrhona® cocoa)

First, temper the dark chocolate to keep it shiny, smooth and stable. Chop the chocolate with a serrated knife and place in an earthenware bowl, then melt it in a bain-marie. Stir gently with a wooden spoon until it reaches 50-55°C. Remove the chocolate from the bain-marie. Place the bowl in a second bowl filled with water and 4-5 ice cubes. Stir the melted chocolate from time to time as it will start to set on the sides of the bowl. As soon as it reaches 27-28°C, return the bowl to the bain-marie, keeping a close eye on the temperature. When it reaches 31-32°C, the chocolate is tempered.

Spread out in a 20 x 10 cm baking frame to approximately 1 cm thick. Using a knife, cut 1 cm strips in one direction and 8 cm strips in the other. Set aside in the fridge. You'll need 20 batons. You can also buy the chocolate batons at the bakery.

FOR THE PISTACHIO ALMOND PASTE
20 g plain shelled pistachios
250 g almond paste (65% almonds)
25 g pistachio paste

On a baking tray lined with greaseproof paper, spread out the shelled pistachios, taking care that they don't overlap. Toast in a fan oven at 150°C for 14 minutes. Leave to cool and then crush them coarsely. In the bowl of a food processor fitted with a flat beater attachment blend all the ingredients. Use immediately.

CUTTING THE PISTACHIO ALMOND PASTE

Using a rolling pin, roll out the almond paste between two sheets of plastic to a thickness of around 1 cm. Cut into rectangles measuring 11 x 7 cm. Place on a sheet of greaseproof paper and wrap in cling film. Set aside in the freezer until ready to use.

FOR THE CROISSANT DOUGH PREPARATION
Croissant dough (the recipe above)
215 g unsalted margarine, at room temperature, 18-19°C

Remove the croissant dough from the fridge. Pound the margarine with a rolling pin to make it smooth and square. On a lightly floured work surface, roll out the dough into a square about twice the size of the margarine.

Pain au chocolat with pistachio

ENCASING AND TURNING

Place the square of margarine in the middle of the dough square and close so that you can no longer see the margarine. Once the margarine is encased, make two simple turns, then place the dough in the fridge for 45 minutes before the third and final simple turn.
Place the dough in the freezer for 1 hour before rolling it out.

ROLLING OUT, DETAILING AND SHAPING

On a lightly floured work surface, roll out the dough to a thickness of around 2.5 mm to obtain a rectangle measuring approximately 32 x 45 cm. Loosen the croissant dough and cut into 10 rectangles, measuring 16 x 9 cm. Place each rectangle of dough with the narrowest side facing you. Place a rectangle of almond paste and a baton of dark chocolate on top. Wrap the pastry around this first baton of chocolate, then add a second baton and finish wrapping loosely to allow the pastry to expand. Arrange the pains au chocolat on a baking tray lined with greaseproof paper and set aside in the fridge for 2 hours.

FOR THE PISTACHIO WATER ICING
250 g icing sugar
50 g still mineral water
12.5 g pistachio paste

Mix the icing sugar, water and pistachio paste and set aside in the fridge.

FOR THE GLAZE
50 g soya milk
15 g maple syrup

Mix the soya milk and maple syrup in a bowl and refrigerate.

FOR FINISHING
Pistachio water icing
60 g extra-green pistachios, peeled and crushed

COOKING AND FINISHING

Remove the tray from the fridge and leave the pains au chocolat to rise for 2-3 hours in a room at 28°C. Preheat the fan oven to 190°C. Brush the pains au chocolat with the glaze, then put them in the oven, lowering the temperature to 170°C and bake for 20-25 minutes, opening the oven door for a few seconds every 8 minutes to let the moisture escape.

Once out of the oven, dip the tops of the pains au chocolat in the pistachio water icing, place them on a wire rack to drain off any excess glaze, then sprinkle with the peeled and crushed extra-green pistachios. Place on a stainless steel rack.

Travel
Cakes

An invitation to escape

As with viennoiseries, cakes, financiers or shortbread also have the delicacy that butter and eggs give them, firstly the taste, and then the melt-in-the-mouth texture. So finding a substitute for these two basic ingredients is no easy task. We had to experiment with different mixes to recreate the texture we love so much in these travel cakes, and then find the right combinations to accompany and develop the flavours.

To create a vegan recipe, you need to start by breaking down the expected actions of conventional ingredients, then bring together those that will mimic their effects. I tried to forget the classic recipes and acquire a new way of thinking in three stages: understanding what gives a traditional cake its structure and taste; familiarising myself with the panoply of vegan ingredients, including natural additives; and analysing the properties of each of them. But at this stage, nothing is set in stone: you have to reinvent the recipes and try out different combinations until you find the one you like. This means that two cake recipes can be completely different.

For butter, it's relatively easy to turn to different vegetable oils chosen according to their melting point. It's also important to find the right proportions and combinations for each recipe. For example, grapeseed oil, which is neutral in flavour, provides the fat, while silken tofu is used for the melt-in-the-mouth texture.

As far as eggs are concerned, it's a tricky business because eggs are the basis of our traditional pâtisserie; they give structure to a mixture. The yolk colours, emulsifies, binds and adds softness to cake batter, while the white helps to hold it in place. All hail the almighty egg! However, it is possible to reproduce the emulsifying properties of the yolk, for example by combining potato protein with water.

For the Ultimate cake, we use a mixture of seeds to adjust the texture and add soya milk and silken tofu for moisture. For the Infinity mandarin cake, however, the combination of ingredients is quite different. It contains potato protein, grapeseed oil and margarine, but no seed mix. For the red berries cake, fruit compote is an alternative. As for the financiers, a mixture of vegetable oils, a vegan milk and ground almonds are required to obtain the desired texture. Each recipe has it's own tailored creation.

When tasted, the pleasurable and intense flavour of these travel cakes are just as enjoyable as the classic recipes.

Infinitely clementine cake

Developing the cakes required a great deal of work to select and assemble the ingredients that give them the soft texture we love about them. Although they are denser and less developed than traditional cakes, the mix of seeds gives them a moist, melt-in-the-mouth texture that's delicious.

Pierre Hermé

Makes 4 cakes

Preparation time: 3 hours
Resting time: 14 hours
Cooking time: 2 hours 40 minutes

FOR THE HOMEMADE SEMI-CONFIT CLEMENTINES (PREPARE THE DAY BEFORE)
2 organic Corsican clementines
500 g still mineral water
250 g caster sugar

Using a serrated knife, cut off both ends of the clementines, then quarter from top to bottom. Blanch them three times in a row by immersing them in plenty of boiling water, leaving to boil for 2 minutes, then rinsing in cold water. Repeat the process twice and drain. Prepare the syrup with the sugar and water and bring to the boil. Add the clementines and simmer over a low heat, covered to preserve their softness, for around 2 hours. Remove and leave to macerate overnight in the fridge before draining with a sieve for 1 hour. Set aside in the fridge.

FOR THE CLEMENTINE SOAKING SYRUP

155 g still mineral water
125 g caster sugar
10 g organic Corsican clementine zest
60 g organic Corsican clementine juice

Bring the water and sugar to the boil in a saucepan, add the clementine zest and leave to stand for 30 minutes, then add the clementine juice. For soaking, the temperature of the syrup should be around 40°C. If it is lower, warm the mixture slightly.

FOR THE CLEMENTINE CAKE MIX

476 g flour
27 g baking powder
5 g Guérande fleur de sel
175 g ground almonds
120 g homemade semi-confit clementine segments
160 g margarine
360 g icing sugar
10 g organic Corsican clementine zest
11 g potato protein
11 g citrus fibre
100 g still mineral water
300 g organic Corsican clementine juice
127 g grapeseed/rapeseed/peanut oil (as preferred)

Sift together the flour and baking powder, then add the fleur de sel and ground almonds. Take a third of this mixture to coat the semi-confit clementine segments. In the bowl of a food processor fitted with a flat beater attachment, combine the margarine, icing sugar and clementine zest. Using an immersion blender, mix the potato protein, citrus fibre, still mineral water and clementine juice. Pour in the oil and blend again to create an emulsion. Pour this mixture into a mixing bowl and whisk. Stir in the flour/baking powder/ground almonds mixture, then the semi-confit clementine segments/flour mixture. Mix and use immediately.

FOR THE MOULDING

Margarine (as needed)
100 g grapeseed/rapeseed/peanut oil (as preferred)

MOULDING AND COOKING

Lightly grease 4 tin cake moulds measuring 14 x 8 cm and 8 cm high and fill with 450 g of cake mix. Using a dough scraper previously dipped in oil, score each cake in the middle and lengthways to encourage them to rise. Bake the cakes in a fan oven at 180°C for 10 minutes, then cook for a further 30 minutes at 160°C. Check the cakes with a paring knife; when they are cooked, turn them out of the tin and place them on a wire rack. Leave to cool for 15 minutes, then proceed with the soaking.

SOAKING

Place the cakes on a wire rack, and then place the latter in a casserole dish or tray. Using a ladle and syrup at around 40°C, soak the cakes three times with the syrup. Leave to drain for 30 minutes before finishing.

FOR THE CLEMENTINE WATER ICING
100 g icing sugar
Zest of 1 organic Corsican clementine
20 g organic Corsican clementine juice
10 g organic lemon juice

Combine all the ingredients and use at 40°C.

FOR FINISHING

Preheat the fan oven to 160°C. Frost the cakes with the clementine water icing and place in the oven for 3 minutes. Allow to cool and then store in the fridge. Remove the cake from the fridge 1 hour before eating.

Ultimate cake

The Ultimate cake blew me away with its pure taste. The vanilla–chocolate duo is more intense, but always perfectly balanced. A little firmer and denser, this cake is infinitely tasty.

Pierre Hermé

Makes 4-5 cakes

Preparation time: 3 hours
Resting time: 1 hour
Cooking time: 1 hour

FOR THE BELIZE CHOCOLATE CUBES WITH FLEUR DE SEL
250 g dark chocolate (Xibun pure Belize 64% Valrhona® cocoa)
5 g Guérande fleur de sel
2 g vanilla powder

Finely crush the fleur de sel crystals with a rolling pin, then sieve through a medium/fine sieve. Set aside the finest crystals.

First, temper the dark chocolate to keep it shiny, smooth and stable. Chop the chocolate with a serrated knife and place in an earthenware bowl, then melt it in a bain-marie. Stir gently with a wooden spoon until it reaches 50-55°C. Remove the chocolate from the bain-marie. Place the bowl in a second bowl filled with water and 4-5 ice cubes. Stir the melted chocolate from time to time as it will start to set on the sides of the bowl. As soon as it reaches 27-28°C, return the bowl to the bain-marie, keeping a close eye on the temperature. When it reaches 31-32°C, the chocolate is tempered. Stir in the vanilla powder and fleur de sel. On a plastic sheet, thinly spread the tempered fleur de sel chocolate to a thickness of about 1 cm. Place a second plastic sheet and a weight on top to prevent the chocolate from warping as it sets. Place in the fridge and leave to set for at least 1 hour. Then, using a knife, cut out 1 cm squares. Separate the squares to prevent them from sticking back together. Leave to set completely and use immediately or store in an airtight container in the fridge.

FOR THE VANILLA SYRUP

325 g still mineral water
250 g caster sugar
1 Madagascar vanilla pod, split and scraped
40 g natural vanilla extract

Bring the ingredients to the boil in a saucepan and leave to infuse for at least 30 minutes. Strain the mixture to obtain the vanilla soaking syrup. The temperature of the syrup should be around 40°C. If it is lower, warm the mixture slightly.

FOR THE HOMEMADE THICKENER MIX

30 g golden flaxseed
17.5 g chia seeds
7.5 g psyllium

Using a food processor, grind the ingredients into a powder and use immediately.

FOR THE VANILLA CAKE MIX

250 g flour
11 g baking powder
2 g Guérande fleur de sel
12.5 g vanilla powder
25 g homemade thickener mix
150 g soya milk
200 g silken tofu
50 g cider vinegar
10 g natural vanilla extract
150 g caster sugar
120 g peanut oil

Sift together the flour and baking powder. Add the fleur de sel, vanilla powder and thickener mix. In the bowl of a food processor fitted with a flat beater attachment, blend the previous mixture with the soya milk, silken tofu, cider vinegar and natural vanilla extract. Blend for 1 minute 30 seconds then add the sugar and blend for 2 minutes. Add the peanut oil and blend for 30 seconds. Use immediately.

FOR THE CHOCOLATE CAKE MIX
200 g flour
11 g baking powder
25 g cocoa powder (Valrhona®)
2 g Guérande fleur de sel
25 g homemade thickener mix
150 g soya milk
200 g silken tofu
50 g cider vinegar
150 g caster sugar
120 g peanut oil

Sift together the flour, baking powder and cocoa powder. Add the fleur de sel and the thickener mix. In the bowl of a food processor fitted with a flat beater attachment, blend the previous mixture with the soya milk, silken tofu and cider vinegar. Blend for 1 minute 30 seconds then add the sugar and blend for 2 minutes. Add the peanut oil and blend for 30 seconds. Use immediately.

FOR THE MOULDING
Margarine (as needed)
100 g grapeseed/rapeseed/peanut oil (as preferred)

MOULDING AND COOKING
Lightly grease 4 tin cake moulds measuring 14 x 8 cm and 8 cm high. Using two piping bags without tips, line the moulds with 100 g of chocolate cake mix, then top with 100 g of vanilla cake mix. Sprinkle with 40 g of Belize chocolate cubes with fleur de sel, then pipe another 75 g of chocolate cake mix, followed by 75 g of vanilla cake mix. Using a dough scraper previously dipped in oil, score each cake in the middle and lengthways to encourage them to rise. Bake the cakes in a fan oven at 160°C for 45 minutes. Check the cakes with a paring knife; when they are cooked, turn them out of the tin and place them on a wire rack. Leave to cool for 15 minutes, then proceed with the soaking.

SOAKING
Place the cakes on a wire rack, and then place the latter in a casserole dish or tray. Using a ladle and syrup at around 40°C, soak the cakes three times with the syrup. Leave to drain well before finishing.

FOR THE DARK CHOCOLATE ICING
200 g black icing paste (Valrhona®)
100 g dark chocolate (Araguani 72% Valrhona® cocoa)
15 g grapeseed oil

In a glass container, melt the icing paste and dark chocolate at 45°C in a bain-marie or in the microwave. Add the grapeseed oil. Transfer to an airtight container and refrigerate. The temperature for use is 40–45°C.

(Cont.)

FOR THE WHITE CHOCOLATE SHARDS WITH VANILLA

100 g white chocolate (Valrhona®)
1 g vanilla powder

First, temper the chocolate to keep it shiny, smooth and stable. Chop the chocolate with a serrated knife and place in an earthenware bowl, then melt it in a bain-marie. Stir gently with a wooden spoon until it reaches 45–50°C. Remove the chocolate from the bain-marie. Place the bowl in a second bowl filled with water and 4-5 ice cubes. Stir the melted chocolate from time to time as it will start to set on the sides of the bowl. As soon as it reaches 26-27°C, return the bowl to the bain-marie, keeping a close eye on the temperature, which should be between 28-29°C. Spread the vanilla white chocolate over a sheet of plastic. Cover with a second plastic sheet and a weight on top to prevent the chocolate from warping as it sets. Store in the fridge.

FOR FINISHING

Melt the dark chocolate icing at 40-45°C using a thermometer or electronic probe. Place the cakes on a wire rack, on top of a casserole dish or tray, and glaze evenly with the dark chocolate icing, taking care to cover each cake completely. Before the icing has completely set, place 2 white chocolate shards with vanilla and 1 dark chocolate shard on top of each cake. Leave to set, then set aside in the fridge. Remove the cakes from the fridge 1 hour before serving. Serve at room temperature.

Strawberry cake

Soft and creamy, the star of this cake is the strawberry, my favourite fruit. To enhance the flavour, it is lightly perfumed with olive oil and lemon zest.

Linda Vongdara

Makes 2 cakes for 6 people

Preparation time: 2 hours
Resting time: 20 minutes
Cooking time: 55 minutes

FOR THE STRAWBERRY MARBLING

200 g strawberry purée
120 g caster sugar
2 g agar-agar powder
20 g potato starch

In a small saucepan, combine all the ingredients and bring to the boil over a low heat. Leave the gel to cool and set aside at room temperature in a piping bag.

FOR THE CRUMBLE

25 g T65 wheat flour or semi-wholegrain rice flour
25 g caster sugar
1 g Guérande fleur de sel
10 g deodorised coconut oil
10 g soya milk

In a small bowl, roughly mix all the ingredients with your fingertips, without warming them or using too much pressure. Put the crumble in the freezer until ready to use.

FOR THE STRAWBERRY CAKE BATTER
15 g flaxseeds
150 g strawberry purée
200 g silken tofu or soya yoghurt
165 g light brown sugar
2 g organic lemon zest
250 g T45 fine wheat flour
10 g baking powder
80 g grapeseed oil
40 g olive oil

In a blender, blend the flaxseeds with the strawberry purée until you obtain a smooth, fine gel. Then add the silken tofu or soya yoghurt, sugar and lemon zest. Blend again. Pour the mixture into a bowl and add the sifted flour in one go. Whisk and leave to stand for at least 20 minutes at room temperature. Once the batter has rested, add the baking powder and emulsify, gradually adding the oils. Whisk until the batter is smooth.

FOR THE MOULDING
60 g whole strawberries

MOULDING AND COOKING

Preheat the fan oven to 170-180°C. Grease and flour 2 14-cm metal cake tins. Pour a third of the cake batter into the tins. Pipe strawberry gel marbling on top, then cover again with cake batter. Repeat this process, alternating the cake batter with the strawberry marbling. Cut the strawberries into large chunks and place them on top, pushing them halfway into the cake batter. Take the crumble out of the freezer and crumble it over. Bake in the oven for 45-50 minutes until golden. Check the cakes are cooked with the tip of a knife. Turn out the warm cakes and leave to cool completely before serving.

Note: in this recipe, the mixture of oil and an ingredient rich in soya protein (tofu or yoghurt) makes the cake soft and gives it a smooth texture. It is important to leave the dough to rest so that the gluten network can form. This results in a supple, melt-in-the-mouth texture after cooking, thanks to the gelling of the starches. In this recipe, gluten and starches are used instead of eggs to hold the cake together, and soya is used as an emulsifier thanks to the lecithin it contains.

Almond financiers

An easy-to-make vegan version of these little almond cakes that can be enjoyed all day long.

Linda Vongdara

Makes 30-40 mini-financiers

Preparation time: 30 minutes
Resting time: 24 hours
Cooking time: 10 minutes

FOR THE ALMOND FINANCIER BATTER (PREPARE THE DAY BEFORE)
50 g deodorised coconut oil
50 g grapeseed oil
160 g soya milk
125 g light brown sugar
150 g T55 wheat flour
5 g baking powder
60 g ground almonds
1 pinch Guérande fleur de sel

Gently melt the deodorised coconut oil in a saucepan over a low heat and mix with the grapeseed oil. Set aside at room temperature.

Place the soya milk in a mixing bowl. Whisk in the light brown sugar until completely dissolved. Sift the flour and baking powder together. Pour this dry mixture in one go into the liquid mixture and combine quickly. Gradually add the ground almonds, fleur de sel and oils to obtain a smooth, emulsified batter. Place the mixture in a piping bag (without tip) and leave to rest for 24 hours in the fridge.

Preheat the fan oven to 240°C. Pipe the batter into round moulds with a diameter of 4 cm. Place in the oven and bake for 5 minutes at 220°C.

Turn out the financiers and place them on a wire rack to cool.

Note: these financiers keep for 5 days in a tin and up to 2 weeks in an airtight container in the fridge.

Quatre temps

I came up with this recipe to celebrate the 30th birthday of my friend Benjamin, a keen traveller. My idea was to make a fruit travel cake, made up of four layers with different flavours and textures, but baked all at once.

Linda Vongdara

Makes 2 cakes for 6 people

Preparation time: 2 hours
Resting time: 24 hours
Cooking time: 1 hour 40 minutes

FOR THE ALMOND FINANCIER BATTER (PREPARE THE DAY BEFORE)

50 g deodorised coconut oil
50 g grapeseed oil
160 g soya milk
125 g light brown sugar
150 g T55 wheat flour
5 g baking powder
60 g ground almonds
1 pinch Guérande fleur de sel

Gently melt the deodorised coconut oil in a saucepan over a low heat and mix with the grapeseed oil. Set aside at room temperature.

Place the soya milk in a mixing bowl. Whisk in the light brown sugar until completely dissolved. Sift the flour and baking powder together. Pour this dry mixture in one go into the liquid mixture and combine quickly. Gradually add the ground almonds, fleur de sel and oils to obtain a smooth, emulsified batter. Place the mixture in a piping bag (without tip) and leave to rest for 24 hours in the fridge.

FOR THE SEMI-DRIED POACHED PEARS

5 small organic pears
250 g caster sugar
500 g still mineral water

Wash the pears. Cut them in half lengthways and remove the core leaving the skin. Place the water and sugar in a saucepan and bring the mixture to the boil. Turn down the heat and place the pears in the syrup for 10 minutes. Preheat the fan oven to 150°C. Using a skimmer, drain the pears and dry them on kitchen paper. Transfer to a baking tray lined with greaseproof paper. Dry them in the oven for 20-30 minutes, then take them out. The pears should be tender and slightly translucent. Leave to cool, then cut each pear half into 4 large pieces and set aside.

TRAVEL CAKES   *An invitation to escape*

FOR THE ALMOND CREAM
200 g soya milk
80 g caster sugar
15 g potato starch
45 g grapeseed oil
110 g ground almonds
½ teaspoon vanilla powder

In a saucepan, whisk together the potato starch and sugar with the soya milk. Leave the mixture to thicken over a low heat. Remove from the heat and whisk in the grapeseed oil, ground almonds and vanilla powder, mixing briskly. Leave the cream to cool and transfer to a piping bag.

FOR THE CRUMBLE
100 g T65 wheat flour or brown rice flour
100 g light brown sugar
80 g cold margarine
50 g chopped almonds or almond sticks
4 g Guérande fleur de sel

Using your fingertips, coarsely mix all the ingredients in a mixing bowl to obtain a crumbly mixture. Set aside in the fridge until ready to use.

ASSEMBLY AND COOKING

Preheat the fan oven to 170°C. Grease 2 rings 16 cm in diameter and 4.5 cm high and place them on a baking tray lined with greaseproof paper. Divide the batter between the two rings. Pipe the almond cream in a spiral shape over the top in an even layer. Place the pear pieces on the almond cream, pressing them in slightly. Top with the crumble. Cook for about 1 hour. When removed from the oven, the cakes should be golden brown. Leave to cool completely, then remove from the rings. Using a sieve, decorate the cakes with a dusting of icing sugar.

Note: the financier batter will be even better if made the day before or 2 days before. These cakes will keep for up to 5 days at room temperature, under a bell jar, or for over a week in the fridge.

Soft chocolate cake

Gluten-free and easy to make, this vegan chocolate cake is both delicious and very light.

Linda Vongdara

Makes 2 cakes for 4-5 people

Preparation time: 1 hour
Resting time: 2 hours
Cooking time: 30 minutes

FOR THE CHOCOLATE CAKE
250 g dark chocolate (72% Valrhona® cocoa)
8 g potato starch
40 g brown sugar
375 g soya milk
22 g grapeseed oil
100 g chestnut flour
55 g ground almonds
3 g baking powder
20 g gold rum
2 g fine salt

First, temper the dark chocolate to keep it shiny, smooth and stable. Chop the chocolate with a serrated knife and place in an earthenware bowl, then melt it in a bain-marie. Stir gently with a wooden spoon until it reaches 50-55°C. Remove the chocolate from the bain-marie. Place the bowl in a second bowl filled with water and 4-5 ice cubes. Stir the melted chocolate from time to time as it will start to set on the sides of the bowl. As soon as it reaches 27-28°C, return the bowl to the bain-marie, keeping a close eye on the temperature which should be 31-32°C.

In a saucepan, whisk together the potato starch, brown sugar and soya milk. Bring the mixture to a simmer over a medium heat, whisking constantly. The mixture will thicken. Remove from the heat and whisk in the dark chocolate and grapeseed oil. The mixture should be smooth, shiny and homogeneous. Sift the chestnut flour and add to the previous mixture. Add the ground almonds, baking powder, rum and salt and mix a final time to blend the mixture. Preheat the fan oven to 180°C. Lightly grease 2 rings 16 cm in diameter and place them on a baking tray lined with greaseproof paper. Pour in the batter and bake the cakes for 12 minutes. Allow to cool before turning out.

FOR THE COCOA MIRROR ICING
125 g caster sugar
9 g pectin NH 95
40 g cocoa powder, 100% degreased
15 g cocoa butter (Valrhona®)
100 g soya milk
100 g still mineral water

Take 2 tablespoons of sugar and mix with the pectin. Place the cocoa powder and cocoa butter in a bowl. Bring the soya milk, water and remaining sugar to the boil in a saucepan. Sprinkle the sugar and pectin mixture into the pan and stir, keeping it boiling over a low heat for a moment until the pectin has completely dissolved. Remove from the heat, pour the hot mixture over the cocoa powder and cocoa butter mixture and emulsify with an immersion blender. Cover the icing with cling film in direct contact and leave to cool.

FOR THE DARK CHOCOLATE TUILES
200 g dark chocolate (72% Valrhona® cocoa)
Cocoa powder (Valrhona® – as needed)

Temper the dark chocolate. To do this, chop it with a serrated knife and then melt it in an earthenware bowl over a bain-marie. Stir gently with a wooden spoon until it reaches 50-55°C. Remove the chocolate from the bain-marie. Place the bowl in a second bowl filled with water and 4-5 ice cubes. Stir the melted chocolate from time to time as it will start to set on the sides of the bowl. As soon as it reaches a temperature of 27-28°C, return the bowl to the bain-marie for a few seconds, keeping a close eye on the temperature. When it reaches 31-32°C, the chocolate is tempered.

On a sheet of greaseproof paper, cut 4 cm wide strips, spread a thin layer of tempered dark chocolate over them, then, using a sieve, sprinkle with cocoa powder before placing the chocolate strip in a log mould. Leave to set at 18°C for 2 hours, then set aside at 18°C until ready to use.

FOR THE ASSEMBLY
Cold cocoa mirror icing (as needed)
50 g cocoa nibs (optional)
2 dark chocolate tuiles

Using an immersion blender, blend the cocoa mirror icing and transfer into a piping bag or paper cone. Pipe spirals with the icing on the surface of the cake. Sprinkle lightly with cocoa nibs and decorate with a chocolate tuile.

Note: in this recipe, pre-cooking the starches contained in the potato starch will allow the cake to absorb more moisture. They will act as a humectant, ensuring that the final texture is softer and more fondant-like.

Breton shortbread

Crunchy and sublime, these thick shortbread biscuits are the perfect vegan treat.

Linda Vongdara

Makes approximately 12 thick biscuits

Preparation time: 30 minutes
Cooking time: 20 minutes

BRETON SHORTBREAD
40 g deodorised coconut oil
40 g grapeseed oil
160 g soya milk
80 g light brown sugar
70 g semi-wholegrain rice flour
30 g potato starch
10 g oat flour or rolled oats, blended to a powder
10 g chickpea flour
10 g baking powder
30 g ground almonds
2 g Guérande fleur de sel

Gently melt the deodorised coconut oil in a saucepan over a low heat and mix with the grapeseed oil. Set aside at room temperature. Place the soya milk and light brown sugar in a mixing bowl and whisk until completely dissolved. Sift together the flours, potato starch and baking powder. Pour this dry mixture all at once into the liquid mixture and whisk quickly to combine. Gradually add the ground almonds, fleur de sel and oils to obtain a smooth, glossy batter.

Preheat the fan oven to 180°C. Lightly grease 12 rings, 7 cm in diameter. Place them on a baking tray covered with greaseproof paper and pour the batter into them. Bake for 15 minutes, until golden brown. Remove from the oven and place on a wire rack to cool completely.

Note: stored in an airtight container at room temperature, these biscuits stay crunchy for 2 weeks.

Spritz

To make this Viennese biscuit, I use a mixture of three gluten-free flours. To make it more indulgent, one side of the biscuit is coated with chocolate. To munch without moderation.

Linda Vongdara

Makes 50 biscuits

Preparation time: 30 minutes
Cooking time: 30 minutes

FOR THE SPRITZ

55 g deodorised coconut oil
100 g grapeseed oil
190 g wholegrain or semi-wholegrain rice flour
100 g oat flour or rolled oats, blended to a powder
20 g chickpea flour
1.5 g baking powder
100 g icing sugar
½ teaspoon vanilla powder
120 g cold still mineral water
2 g Guérande fleur de sel

Gently melt the deodorised coconut oil in a saucepan over a low heat and mix with the grapeseed oil. Set aside at room temperature. Put the flours and baking powder in the bowl of a food processor fitted with a flat beater attachment. Add the oils and process until the mixture has a creamy texture. Pour in the icing sugar, add the vanilla powder and mix again to obtain a smooth texture. Moisten the resulting batter by adding the water gradually while continuing to mix to emulsify it and obtain a creamy texture that holds together. It is not always necessary to use the full quantity of water. Add the fleur de sel, run the food processor for a few moments and then transfer the batter to a piping bag fitted with a 13 mm fluted tip. Preheat the fan oven to 180°C. On a baking tray covered with a non-stick silicone mat, pipe the spritz in small, tight zigzags. Bake for 25 minutes, until golden brown. Leave the spritz to cool completely on a wire rack.

FOR THE CHOCOLATE GLAZE

100 g dark chocolate (72% Valrhona® cocoa)
100 g cocoa butter (Valrhona®)

Melt the dark chocolate and cocoa butter in a bain-marie. When the texture is sufficiently thick, dip the spritz halfway into the glaze and leave to cool on a sheet of greaseproof paper. Store in an airtight container.

Little Flos with almonds

This recipe was inspired by my friend Florent, known as 'Flo', whose favourite dessert is flan. He came up with the idea of using oilseed purée to make the creamy base.

Linda Vongdara

Makes 10-12 individual flans

Preparation time: 1 hour 30 minutes
Resting time: 20 minutes
Cooking time: 40-50 minutes

FOR THE SWEET SHORTCRUST PASTRY
138 g T55 wheat flour
38 g potato starch
61 g icing sugar
23 g ground almonds
3 g Guérande fleur de sel
46 g cocoa butter (Valrhona®)
19 g grapeseed oil
61 g soya milk
A little cocoa butter to coat the pastry

Mix the flour, potato starch, icing sugar, ground almonds and fleur de sel in the bowl of a food processor fitted with a flat beater attachment. Melt the cocoa butter in a small saucepan or in the microwave. Mix it with the grapeseed oil, then pour the mixture into the food processor bowl. Process on medium speed, until the fat is absorbed by the dry ingredients. Pour in the soya milk gradually, stirring constantly until the texture is smooth. Cover the pastry with cling film and place in the fridge for at least 20 minutes to firm up. Take the pastry out of the fridge and roll out to a thickness of 2-3 mm between 2 sheets of greaseproof paper. Prick the pastry with a fork and line 10-12 pastry rings 6 cm in diameter and 2.5 cm high. Place the pastry shells in the freezer for 20 minutes. Preheat the fan oven to 180°C. Remove the pastry shells from the freezer and line them with aluminium foil topped with pie weights or dried beans. Place in the oven for 15-20 minutes, remove the foil, pie weights or dried beans and finish cooking for 5-10 minutes at 170°C until golden brown all over. When they come out of the oven, brush a little melted cocoa butter around the inside of the pastry shells to keep them crisp. Set aside at room temperature.

(Cont.)

FOR THE FLAN MIXTURE
110 g light brown sugar
15 g potato starch
15 g cornstarch
1 g agar-agar powder
250 g oat milk
180 g soya milk
100 g white almond butter
80 g deodorised coconut oil

In a saucepan, make a dry mixture with the sugar, potato starch, cornflour and agar-agar. Combine this mixture with the oat and soya milk. Bring everything to the boil. Remove from the heat and emulsify the hot mixture by adding the white almond butter and deodorised coconut oil while mixing with an immersion blender. Fill the baked pastry shells to the brim with this mixture. Set the fan oven to 200°C on grill mode and grill the flans for about 5 minutes until golden brown. Leave to cool completely before serving.

Pear and caramel moffa

Baking this cake in a cloud of steam gives it an incomparable softness. It can be enjoyed warm and with fruit, caramel or chocolate.

Linda Vongdara

Serves 6

Preparation time: 1 hour
Resting time: 2 hours
Cooking time: 1 hour

FOR THE CARAMELISED PEARS
3 firm pears
700 g caster sugar
300 g hot water

Peel, halve and core the pears. Preheat the fan oven to 170°C. Make a dry caramel with the sugar. When the caramel is amber-brown, stir in the hot water to dilute it. Pour the liquid caramel into an ovenproof dish and place the pears in the caramel. Cover the dish with aluminium foil and place the pears in the oven for 40 minutes, turning halfway through cooking. Allow the pears to cool in the caramel. Set aside 180 g of cooking caramel for the whipped ganache.

FOR THE ALMOND AND CARAMEL WHIPPED GANACHE

1 Madagascar vanilla pod
120 g soya milk
10 g inverted sugar
180 g cooking caramel from the pears
170 g white almond butter (unsweetened)
60 g cocoa butter (Valrhona®)
40 g margarine
160 g oat milk
3 g Guérande fleur de sel

Split the vanilla pod in half and scrape out the seeds with a knife. In a saucepan, heat the soya milk, inverted sugar and caramel together until the caramel has completely dissolved. Remove from the heat and add the white almond butter, cocoa butter and finely diced margarine. Emulsify the mixture with an immersion blender until smooth and shiny. Add the oat milk and fleur de sel and blend again. Refrigerate the ganache for at least 2 hours. Whip the chilled ganache until stiff. Set aside in the fridge.

FOR THE MOFFA

200 g soya yoghurt
60 g light brown sugar
60 g plain flour
40 g potato starch
5 g baking powder
150 g dried biscuits (or leftovers of vegan sweet shortcrust pastry...)
70 g grapeseed oil

Place the soya yoghurt and light brown sugar in a bowl and whisk until the sugar has completely dissolved.

Crush the biscuits to a powder and set aside 25 g to line a 16 cm diameter tin. Sift together the flour, potato starch and baking powder and add to the crushed biscuits to make a dry mixture. Add the dry mixture to the sweetened yoghurt and whisk until smooth. Quickly whisk in the oil in a thin stream, as you would a mayonnaise.

Lightly grease the inside of the tin and line with a thin layer of biscuit powder. Pour in the mixture and place the tin in a steamer basket. Cook for 15-20 minutes with constant steam. Check the moffa with a paring knife, the blade should come out clean. Cook for longer if necessary. Leave the cake to cool in the tin, then turn it out and place on a wire rack to cool.

Note: moffa is a very moist steamed yoghurt cake. The batter is enriched with crushed biscuits to give it extra flavour and a subtle biscuity taste. This recipe allows you to recycle leftover sweet shortcrust pastry or cake cuttings that have been dried and roasted in the oven. You can also use bought speculoos with no ingredients of animal origin.

Steamed chocolate fondant

For this recipe, I wanted to create a dessert that was rich in chocolate, very indulgent and would melt in the mouth. I chose to use a gentle steaming process.

Linda Vongdara

Makes 2 cakes for 4-5 people

Preparation time: 1 hour
Resting time: 2 hours
Cooking time: 30 minutes

FOR THE STEAMED CHOCOLATE FONDANT
120 g soya milk
60 g caster sugar
200 g dark chocolate (62% Valrhona® cocoa)
70 g grapeseed oil
70 g plain flour
40 g potato starch
5 g baking powder

Mix the soya milk with the sugar until it has completely dissolved. In a saucepan, over a low heat or bain-marie, gently melt the dark chocolate with the grapeseed oil. When the chocolate has melted, remove from the heat and whisk in the sweetened soya milk. Sift together the flour, potato starch and baking powder. Add this dry mixture to the liquid mixture and whisk until smooth. Grease 2 rings or moulds 16 cm in diameter and pour in the batter. Steam for 15-20 minutes so as not to overcook the core, which should remain gooey while still warm. Allow to cool completely before turning out.

FOR THE CHOCOLATE, HAZELNUT AND CARAMEL GANACHE

160 g oat milk
160 g soya milk
10 g inverted sugar
½ Tahiti vanilla pod
40 g margarine
170 g roasted Piedmont hazelnut butter (sugar-free)
120 g almond milk chocolate (Amatika 46% Valrhona® cocoa)
140 g caster sugar
3 g Guérande fleur de sel

In a saucepan, combine the oat milk, soya milk and inverted sugar. Split the vanilla pod in half and scrape out the seeds. Put the vanilla in the vegan milks/inverted sugar mixture and add the margarine. Bring everything to the boil. Remove from the heat, cover the pan and leave the mixture to infuse for 15 minutes, then remove the vanilla half-pod. Place the chocolate and hazelnut butter in a mixing bowl and set aside. In another saucepan, use the sugar to make a dry caramel. When it turns an amber colour, gradually add the hot vegan milks/inverted sugar/margarine mixture and mix well. When the mixture is smooth, pour it over the chocolate and hazelnut butter. Emulsify with an immersion blender and add the fleur de sel. Cover the ganache with cling film in direct contact, leave the mixture to cool, then place in the fridge for at least 2 hours.

FOR THE COCOA MIRROR ICING

125 g caster sugar
9 g pectin NH 95
40 g cocoa powder, 100% degreased
15 g cocoa butter (Valrhona®)
100 g soya milk
100 g still mineral water

Take 2 tablespoons of sugar and mix with the pectin. Place the cocoa powder and cocoa butter in a bowl. Bring the soya milk, water and remaining sugar to the boil in a saucepan. Sprinkle the sugar and pectin mixture into the pan and stir, keeping it boiling over a low heat for a moment until the pectin has completely dissolved. Remove from the heat, pour the hot mixture over the cocoa powder and cocoa butter mixture and emulsify with an immersion blender. Cover the icing with cling film in direct contact and leave to cool.

FOR THE ASSEMBLY AND FINISHING
200 g cocoa mirror icing

Place the chocolate, hazelnut and caramel ganache in a piping bag fitted with a small Saint Honoré tip. Pipe the ganache in parallel lines over the entire surface of the fondant. Blend the cocoa mirror icing to make it smooth and supple, then place it in a piping bag. Dot a little of the glossy icing between the lines of ganache. Keep the fondants in the fridge and take them out 15 minutes before serving.

Note: the steaming process gives a melt-in-the-mouth, molten texture and preserves all the chocolate flavours.

Chocolate desserts and bonbons

Chocolate addict

With chocolate, the difference in taste and texture between vegan and traditional cakes is more subtle, and they're quite difficult to differentiate. Although, once again, what I'm looking for is the sheer pleasure of taste, not the comparison. However, it has to be said that our palates have appreciated the contribution of animal fats for decades, so it's difficult not to refer to them almost instinctively when tasting.

In a recipe, butter is used, among other things, as a flavour carrier and its taste has an impact on that of the ingredient you want to showcase, in this case chocolate. By removing the butter, the taste of the chocolate is expressed differently, in a clearer, purer way.

When used in the right balance, vegetable oils and vegan milks can create a wide variety of textures, including ganache, mousse, pastries and biscuit. The range of flavours in vegan milks — oat, soya, rice, coconut, almond — as well as in oils, is also a great asset. Non-dairy cream, on the other hand, is reserved for recipes in which we are looking for a fat that is more neutral in taste.

For the pastries, we've adapted the recipes using margarine, vegetable oils and flour blends, each chosen for its flavour and the structure it can add to the pastry. The compositions are sometimes more complex because they involve combining several elements. The textures are also different, often firmer and crunchier but always tasty and extremely good.

In these vegan creations, chocolate reveals its secrets: it is more intense, more distinct and closer to its original taste.

Chocolate and buckwheat tart

I wanted to make this a gluten-free tart, so I chose buckwheat to make a unique recipe. Then it's all about the contrasting textures of the crunchy vegan pastry, the buckwheat praline and the silky ganache.

Pierre Hermé

Makes 2 tarts for 6-8 people

Preparation time: 6 hours
Resting time: 12 hours
Cooking time: 1 hour 30 minutes

FOR THE SWEET BUCKWHEAT PASTRY
45 g deodorised coconut oil
45 g cocoa butter (Valrhona®)
80 g ground almonds
2 g Guérande fleur de sel
110 g icing sugar
55 g still mineral water
220 g buckwheat flour

Melt the deodorised coconut oil and cocoa butter at 30-35°C, checking using a thermometer or electronic probe. Pour the ground almonds, fleur de sel and icing sugar into the bowl of a food processor fitted with a flat beater attachment, then add the coconut oil and cocoa butter mixture, melted at 30°C. Blend until well incorporated, then add the water (heated to 40°C). Add the buckwheat flour. Place on a baking tray, cover with cling film in direct contact and refrigerate for 2 hours.

On a lightly floured work surface, roll out the pastry to a thickness of around 2-3 mm. Using a 27 cm ring, cut out 2 discs of pastry. Place on a baking tray in the fridge for 30 minutes before baking. Grease 2 stainless steel rings 21 cm in diameter and 2 cm high, line them with the pastry and trim off any excess. Refrigerate for 1 hour before placing in the freezer for at least 2 hours. Preheat the fan oven to 250°C. Just before placing in the oven, lower the temperature to 170°C. Place the pastry shells on a baking tray lined with greaseproof paper, line with aluminium foil or greaseproof paper and fill with dried beans. Bake at 170°C for about 25 minutes. Remove from the oven and allow to cool, then remove the dried beans and foil.

(Cont.)

FOR THE TOASTED BUCKWHEAT SEEDS

350 g buckwheat seeds

On a baking tray lined with greaseproof paper, spread out the buckwheat seeds, taking care that they don't overlap. Place in a fan oven at 160°C for 15 minutes until the seeds are golden brown and crunchy. Leave to cool.

FOR THE HOMEMADE ALMOND AND BUCKWHEAT PRALINE

125 g caster sugar
40 g still mineral water
100 g whole white almonds
100 g toasted buckwheat seeds
40 g grapeseed oil
1.5 g Guérande fleur de sel

On a baking tray lined with greaseproof paper, spread out the almonds, taking care that they don't overlap. Bake in a fan oven at 160 °C for 15 minutes. Cook the sugar and water in a saucepan until a thermometer or electronic probe reads 121°C. Pour the hot syrup over the warm toasted almonds and buckwheat seeds. Mix gently with a wooden spatula, then leave to caramelise over a medium heat. Transfer to a non-stick silicone mat to cool. When cool, coarsely chop and add to the bowl of a food processor. Add the fleur de sel and grapeseed oil, and blend until you obtain a paste that should not be too finely ground. Set aside in the fridge.

Note: caramelised almonds must be crushed, ground and used as soon as they have cooled. Once they have been caramelised, they must not be stored as they can absorb moisture and this would alter the quality of the praline.

FOR THE DARK CHOCOLATE GANACHE

400 g dark chocolate (Ampamakia 64% Valrhona® cocoa)
320 g oat milk
60 g inverted sugar
80 g glucose syrup
2 g citrus fibre
50 g deodorised coconut oil

Chop the chocolate. In a saucepan, bring the oat milk, inverted sugar, glucose syrup and citrus fibre to the boil, then pour over the chopped chocolate in three batches. Stir starting from the centre and working outwards. Add the deodorised coconut oil and, using an immersion blender, blend to emulsify. Place in a casserole dish, cover with cling film in direct contact and leave to cool and set in the fridge for around 12 hours before use.

FOR THE NOUGATINE WITH COCOA NIBS AND BUCKWHEAT

50 g still mineral water
50 g glucose syrup
150 g caster sugar
2.5 g pectin NH
65 g rapeseed or grapeseed oil
2.5 g citrus fibre
50 g cocoa nibs
100 g toasted buckwheat seeds
1 g Guérande fleur de sel

In a saucepan, heat the water and glucose syrup to 45-50°C, checking using a thermometer or electronic probe. Add the sugar and pectin NH and heat to 106°C, checking using a thermometer or electronic probe. Add the oil and citrus fibre and blend using an immersion blender. Add the cocoa nibs, buckwheat seeds and fleur de sel. Divide the nougatine between two sheets of greaseproof paper and spread with a palette knife. Cover with another sheet of greaseproof paper and continue to spread by pressing with a rolling pin over the sheets. Wrap in cling film and freeze for at least 2 hours. Cut the still-frozen sheets in half and place each half on a baking tray lined with a non-stick silicone mat. Cook in a fan oven at 170°C for 18-20 minutes. Leave to cool and use immediately or store in an airtight container at room temperature.

(Cont.)

FOR THE BUCKWHEAT CRUMBLE

72 g deodorised coconut oil
96 g ground almonds
2 g Guérande fleur de sel
72 g caster sugar
92 g buckwheat flour
26 g still mineral water
20 g toasted buckwheat seeds

Melt the deodorised coconut oil at 30–35°C, checking using a thermometer or electronic probe. Place the ground almonds, fleur de sel, sugar and sifted buckwheat flour in the bowl of a food processor fitted with a flat beater attachment, then pour in the coconut oil, melted at 30°C. Blend until well incorporated, then add the water (heated to 40°C) and the toasted buckwheat seeds. Transfer to a baking tray and refrigerate for 2 hours. Press through a very large-holed sieve; store in an airtight container in the fridge or freezer. Spread the crumble out on a baking tray lined with greaseproof paper taking care that it doesn't overlap. Put the tray in the fan oven at 160°C and bake for around 20 minutes until the crumble is golden brown. Leave to cool.

ASSEMBLY AND FINISHING

Fill each pastry shell with around 160 g of homemade almond and buckwheat praline, sprinkle with toasted buckwheat seeds and then top with dark chocolate ganache up to the level of the sweet shortcrust pastry shell. Leave to set in the fridge. Once the ganache has set, sprinkle with the remaining toasted buckwheat seeds, then top with the crumble and nougatine shards. Keep in the fridge until ready to use.

Infinitely pure origin Ecuador chocolate tart

My aim with this tart was to rediscover the density and depth of Hacienda Eleonor pure origin chocolate from Ecuador, made by my friend Pierre-Yves Comte. The chocolate is combined with the lightness of a chantilly made from whipped chocolate and oat milk. I love the contrasting textures and the purity of flavour.

Pierre Hermé

Makes 2 tarts for 6-8 people

Preparation time: 6 hours
Resting time: 14 hours
Cooking time: 45 minutes

FOR THE PURE ORIGIN ECUADOR DARK CHOCOLATE GANACHE (PREPARE THE DAY BEFORE)

400 g dark chocolate (Hacienda Eleonor pure origin Ecuador 64% Valrhona® cocoa)
320 g oat milk
60 g inverted sugar
80 g glucose syrup
2 g citrus fibre
50 g deodorised coconut oil

Chop the dark chocolate. In a saucepan, bring the oat milk, inverted sugar, glucose syrup and citrus fibre to the boil, then pour over the chopped chocolate in three batches. Stir starting from the centre and working outwards. Add the deodorised coconut oil and, using an immersion blender, blend to emulsify. Place in a casserole dish, cover with cling film in direct contact and leave to cool and set in the fridge for around 12 hours.

FOR THE PURE ORIGIN ECUADOR CHOCOLATE CHANTILLY (PREPARE THE DAY BEFORE)
335 g oat milk
200 g dark chocolate (Hacienda Eleonor Pure Origin Ecuador 64% Valrhona® cocoa)

Chop the dark chocolate. Bring the oat milk to the boil in a saucepan, then pour over the chocolate. Stir starting from the centre and working outwards. Using an immersion blender, blend everything together. Place in a casserole dish, cover with cling film in direct contact and leave to cool and set in the fridge for around 12 hours.

FOR THE SWEET SHORTCRUST PASTRY
35 g deodorised coconut oil
35 g cocoa butter (Valrhona®)
80 g ground almonds
2 g Guérande fleur de sel
90 g icing sugar
75 g still mineral water
235 g flour

Melt the deodorised coconut oil and cocoa butter at 30-35°C, checking using a thermometer or electronic probe. Pour the ground almonds, fleur de sel and icing sugar into the bowl of a food processor fitted with a flat beater attachment, then add the coconut oil and cocoa butter mixture at 30°C. Blend until well incorporated, then add the water (heated to 40°C). Add the sifted flour. Place on a baking tray, cover with cling film in direct contact and refrigerate for 2 hours.

On a lightly floured work surface, roll out the pastry to a thickness of around 2-3 mm. Using rings, cut out 10 discs 12 cm in diameter. Place on a baking tray in the fridge for 30 minutes before baking. Grease 10 stainless steel rings 8 cm in diameter and 2 cm high, line them with the pastry and trim off any excess. Refrigerate for 1 hour before placing in the freezer for at least 2 hours. Preheat the fan oven to 250°C. Just before placing in the oven, lower the temperature to 170°C. Place the pastry shells on a baking tray lined with greaseproof paper, line with aluminium foil or greaseproof paper and fill with dried beans. Bake at 170°C for about 20 minutes. Remove from the oven and allow to cool, then remove the dried beans and foil. Keep the stainless steel rings for the rest of the assembly.

FOR THE CRUNCHY PRALINE WITH COCOA NIBS
22 g deodorised coconut oil
48 g pure cocoa paste (100% Valrhona® cocoa)
192 g almond praline (60% almonds)
40 g cocoa nibs (Valrhona®)

Melt the deodorised coconut oil and pure cocoa paste at 45°C, checking using a thermometer or electronic probe. Put the almond praline in a mixing bowl, then mix with the melted deodorised coconut oil and pure cocoa paste, and the cocoa nibs. Use immediately or set aside to assemble the tarts.

FOR THE CHOCOLATE SPONGE
37.5 g flour
37.5 g potato starch
5 g baking powder
25 g cocoa powder (Valrhona®)
10 g potato protein
0.37 g xanthan gum
125 g still mineral water
125 g caster sugar
25 g sunflower/rapeseed/grapeseed oil (as preferred)

Sift together the flour, potato starch, baking powder and cocoa powder. Using an immersion blender, mix the potato protein, xanthan gum and water. In the bowl of a food processor fitted with a whisk attachment, whip the mixture, gradually adding the sugar until the mixture is stiff, then drizzle in the oil and blend gently for a few more seconds. Stop the food processor, remove the bowl and using a spatula, gently fold the sifted dry ingredients into the mixture. Use immediately. On a baking tray lined with greaseproof paper, spread the chocolate sponge batter. Cook in a fan oven at 180°C for around 14 minutes. After removing from the oven, leave to cool on a wire rack.

FOR THE CHOCOLATE SOAKING SYRUP
100 g still mineral water
100 g caster sugar
25 g pure cocoa paste (100% Valrhona® cocoa)

Chop the pure cocoa paste using a serrated knife. In a saucepan, bring the water and sugar to the boil, then add the chopped pure cocoa paste and blend using an immersion blender. Use immediately.

CHOCOLATE SPONGE CAKE AND CHOCOLATE SOAKING SYRUP

Heat the chocolate soaking syrup to around 40°C, checking using a thermometer or electronic probe. Using a pastry brush, generously soak the chocolate sponge cake in the syrup, then leave to rest in the fridge for 30 minutes. Using an 18 cm diameter stainless steel ring, cut out 2 discs and set aside to assemble the tart.

CHOCOLATE CHANTILLY AND SOAKED CHOCOLATE SPONGE CAKE DISCS

In the bowl of a food processor fitted with a flat beater attachment, whip the chocolate chantilly. On a stainless steel baking tray covered with a non-stick silicone mat, place a silicone mould with two cavities, 20 cm in diameter and 1.5 cm high. Pipe the chantilly cream three quarters of the way up, then place the soaked sponge disc on top and smooth it down so the mould is filled to the brim. Freeze for 4 hours until the discs are hard. Once frozen, remove the silicone moulds and place the discs in cling film in the freezer to assemble the tarts.

FOR THE DARK CHOCOLATE GLAZE

92 g dark chocolate (Hacienda Eleonor Pure Origin Ecuador 64% Valrhona® cocoa)
150 g neutral glaze
55 g still mineral water
1.5 g caster sugar
1.6 g pectin X58
17 g deodorised coconut oil
0.3 g liquid sunflower lecithin

Melt the chocolate in a bain-marie. In a saucepan, melt the neutral glaze at around 40°C, checking using a thermometer or electronic probe. Heat the water to 40°C, checking using a thermometer or electronic probe. Whisk the sugar and pectin into the water, then bring to the boil. Add the deodorised coconut oil and, using an immersion blender, blend the mixture. Pour over the melted neutral glaze and stir. Pour over the melted chocolate and add the lecithin. Blend to obtain a smooth glaze. Use immediately, or store in an airtight container in the fridge.

FOR THE DARK CHOCOLATE DECORATION

200 g dark chocolate (Hacienda Eleonor Pure Origin Ecuador 64% Valrhona® cocoa)
Cocoa powder (Valrhona® – as needed)

First, temper the dark chocolate to keep it shiny, smooth and stable. To do this, chop it with a serrated knife and then melt it in an earthenware bowl over a bain-marie. Stir gently with a wooden spoon until it reaches 50-55°C. Remove the chocolate from the bain-marie. Place the bowl in a second bowl filled with water and 4-5 ice cubes. Stir the melted chocolate from time to time as it will start to set on the sides of the bowl. As soon as it reaches 27-28°C, return the bowl to the bain-marie for a few seconds, keeping a close eye on the temperature, which should be 31-32°C.

On a sheet of greaseproof paper, cut 4 cm wide strips, spread a thin layer of tempered chocolate over them, then, using a sieve, sprinkle with cocoa powder before placing the chocolate strip in a log mould. Leave to set at 18°C for 2 hours, then set aside at 18°C until ready to use.

ASSEMBLY AND FINISHING

Spread 160 g of crunchy praline with cocoa nibs over the sweet shortcrust pastry base, then fill to the top with chocolate ganache. Leave to set in the fridge for 1-2 hours. Separately, place the disc of chantilly and soaked chocolate sponge cake on a wire rack and coat with the dark chocolate glaze at 40°C, smoothing the top with a palette knife. Place it gently on top of the set ganache. Add 6 dark chocolate shards. Keep in the fridge until ready to use.

Royal chocolate praline

The Royal is a traditional, rich chocolate cake. In this gluten-free version, I wanted to add more lightness while retaining the intensity of the chocolate.

Linda Vongdara

Makes 12 individual cakes

Preparation time: 2 hours
Resting time: 3 hours
Cooking time: 25 minutes

FOR THE SOFT BISCUIT
80 g deodorised coconut oil
80 g grapeseed oil
160 g soya milk
½ teaspoon lemon juice
160 g caster sugar
20 g chickpea flour
20 g oat flour
140 g semi-wholegrain rice flour
60 g potato starch
16 g baking powder
60 g ground toasted hazelnuts
1 pinch Guérande fleur de sel
100 g melted chocolate to coat the biscuit

Melt the deodorised coconut oil in a small saucepan over a low heat. Mix with the grapeseed oil and set aside at room temperature. Mix the soya milk and lemon juice in a mixing bowl. Add the caster sugar and whisk to dissolve in the liquid. Sift together the flours, potato starch and baking powder and add to the liquid mixture, mixing well. Leave the dough for at least 20 minutes. Gradually add the oils and whisk to emulsify, as if making mayonnaise. Finish by stirring in the ground hazelnuts and the fleur de sel. The dough must be smooth. Preheat the fan oven to 200°C. Pour the biscuit dough onto a baking tray lined with greaseproof paper. Smooth the surface with an offset spatula, then bake for 10 minutes. The biscuit should be golden brown. Leave it to cool, then cut out 12 discs with a 5 cm diameter biscuit cutter. Coat them with a thin layer of chocolate that has been melted in the microwave. Set aside in the fridge for assembly.

Dry the biscuit offcuts in the oven at 170°C for 10 minutes until they are completely dry and golden, like crispbread. These dried biscuit offcuts will be used for the praline crunch.

FOR THE PRALINE CRUNCH

50 g dried crisp biscuit offcuts
65 g dark chocolate (64% Valrhona® cocoa)
12 g deodorised coconut oil
250 g praline (50% almonds and 50% hazelnuts)
60 g pure hazelnut paste (100% hazelnuts)
3 g Guérande fleur de sel

Crush the biscuits with a rolling pin. Melt the chocolate with the deodorised coconut oil in a bain-marie, then add the praline, pure hazelnut paste, fleur de sel and crisp biscuit offcuts. Mix well. Pour the mixture into 5 cm diameter moulds or rings and place the coated biscuits on top. Freeze until assembly.

FOR THE CHOCOLATE MOUSSE

300 g dark chocolate (64% Valrhona® cocoa)
15 g cornflour
2.5 g agar-agar powder
400 g oat milk
125 g soya milk
180 g margarine
60 g yumgo white powder
40 g caster sugar

12 stainless steel moulds or rings 6.5 cm in diameter and 4.5 cm high

Chop the chocolate. In a saucepan, whisk together the cornflour, agar-agar and vegan milks. Bring the mixture to the boil while whisking, then pour over the dark chocolate to melt. Add the margarine and emulsify with an immersion blender. Allow the mixture to cool to 35°C, then whisk the yumgo, adding the sugar gradually until it forms stiff peaks. Whisk a third of the whipped yumgo/sugar into the chocolate mixture, then gradually add the rest, mixing the mousse gently with the whisk from top to bottom so that it doesn't fall. On a baking tray lined with greaseproof paper, place 12 stainless steel moulds or rings, 6.5 cm in diameter and 4.5 cm high, lined with a plastic strip. Fill them three-quarters full with mousse. Spread the mousse around the edges using a small spatula. Turn out the soft, crunchy praline biscuit inserts and place them on top of the mousse. They should reach the top of the moulds or rings. Freeze for at least 2 hours.

(Cont.)

FOR THE COCOA MIRROR ICING
250 g caster sugar
18 g pectin NH 95
80 g cocoa powder, 100% degreased
30 g cocoa butter (Valrhona®)
200 g still mineral water

Take 2 tablespoons of sugar and mix with the pectin. Place the cocoa powder and cocoa butter in a bowl. Bring the soya milk, water and remaining sugar to the boil in a saucepan. Sprinkle the sugar and pectin mixture into the pan and stir, keeping it boiling over a low heat for a moment until the pectin has completely dissolved. Remove from the heat, pour the hot mixture over the cocoa powder and cocoa butter mixture and emulsify with an immersion blender. Cover the icing with cling film in direct contact and leave to cool, mixing regularly. When the glaze reaches 40°C, it is ready to use.

ASSEMBLY AND FINISHING
150 g praline (50% almonds and 50% hazelnuts)
18 whole toasted hazelnuts with their skins

Take the chocolate mousses out of the freezer, turn out from the moulds or rings. Place them on a wire rack over a container to catch any excess icing. Stick them on skewers and dip them in the mirror icing. Return them to the rack and leave to set. When the icing has set, place a little praline on top. Garnish with halved hazelnuts and hazelnut skins. Leave to defrost completely in the fridge and keep refrigerated until ready to use.

Note: if you have any leftover mirror icing, keep it in the fridge — it will keep for 15 days. This icing can also be used to decorate the soft chocolate cake (page 63) and the steamed chocolate fondant (page 76).

Fleur de cassis dessert

I came up with this dessert in 2020 when I was working with Nicolas Cloiseau. The starting point was the Noir de cassis ganache, my favourite at La Maison du Chocolat. This combination of flavours inspired me to create Fleur de cassis. It offers a multitude of textures and tastes amplified by the absence of animal fats.

Pierre Hermé

Serves 6-8

Preparation time: 6 hours
Resting time: 12 hours
Cooking time: 45 minutes

FOR THE GLUTEN-FREE FLOUR MIX
100 g semi-wholegrain rice flour
60 g cornflour
20 g potato starch
20 g ground almonds

Sift together all the ingredients

FOR THE BLACKCURRANT PEPPER CRUMBLE

70 g margarine
70 g light brown sugar
70 g gluten-free flour mix
0.15 g blackcurrant pepper, a small pinch
0.15 g Guérande fleur de sel, a small pinch
55 g ground almonds
15 g cornflour

In the bowl of the mixer fitted with a flat beater attachment introduce and mix the ingredients in order. Cover with cling film and refrigerate for 2 hours. On a lightly floured work surface, using a rolling pin, roll out the crumble dough to a thickness of about 5 mm. Prick the dough with a fork and bake in a preheated fan oven at 165°C for 25 minutes. Remove from the oven. Using a stainless steel ring, cut out a disc 18 cm in diameter.

FOR THE CHOCOLATE BISCUIT

90 g gluten-free flour mix
12 g baking powder
40 g cocoa powder
10 g potato protein
1.5 g xanthan gum
300 g still mineral water
170 g caster sugar
85 g ground almonds
100 g grapeseed oil

Sift together the gluten-free flour mixture, baking powder and cocoa powder. Using an immersion blender, mix the potato protein, xanthan gum and water. Blend on medium speed for about 1 minute, then add the sugar and blend for a further 30 seconds. Add the sifted flours/baking powder mixture and the ground almonds, mixing with a spatula, then drizzle in the grapeseed oil.

Spread the biscuit evenly on a baking tray lined with greaseproof paper. Cook in a fan oven at 170°C for around 20 minutes. Leave to cool and cut out a disc 18 cm in diameter.

FOR THE CHOCOLATE AND BLACKCURRANT GANACHE

100 g dark chocolate (Hacienda Eleonor Pure Origin Ecuador 64% Valrhona® cocoa)
100 g blackcurrant purée
20 g redcurrant purée
50 g still mineral water
10 g fresh lemon juice
1 g blackcurrant pepper
40 g margarine

Melt the chocolate in the microwave or in a bain-marie. In a saucepan, heat the blackcurrant purée, redcurrant purée, water, lemon juice and blackcurrant pepper. Gradually stir this mixture into the melted chocolate. The mixture should be smooth, homogeneous, creamy and light. Leave to cool. When the ganache reaches around 40°C, gently stir in the margarine using a spatula. Blend with an immersion blender. Leave to cool slightly and use.

FOR THE BLACKCURRANT COMPOTE
110 g blackcurrant purée
20 g redcurrant purée
20 g caster sugar
4 g pectin NH

Heat the purées in a saucepan to 50°C, add a mixture of the pectin and sugar and bring to the boil. Leave to cool in the fridge before use.

FOR THE CHOCOLATE BISCUIT DISC, CHOCOLATE AND BLACKCURRANT GANACHE AND BLACKCURRANT COMPOTE
50 g blackcurrants in syrup

Place an 18 cm diameter pastry ring on a stainless steel baking tray lined with greaseproof paper. Place the chocolate biscuit disc in the ring and spread with the chocolate and blackcurrant ganache. Leave to set in the fridge and then freeze so that you can turn the disc over. On the other side of the biscuit, pour and spread the blackcurrant compote, then sprinkle with 50 g of blackcurrants in syrup. Freeze for 3 hours and store in the freezer wrapped in cling film until assembly.

FOR THE DARK CHOCOLATE MOUSSE
170 g still mineral water
5 g potato protein
2 g xanthan gum
270 g dark chocolate (Hacienda Eleonor Pure Origin Ecuador 64% Valrhona® cocoa)
10 g caster sugar
6 g cornflour
185 g oat milk
5 g deodorised coconut oil

Using an immersion blender, mix the water, potato protein and xanthan gum. Leave to rest for 20 minutes in the fridge before whipping the mixture at medium speed in the bowl of a food processor fitted with a whisk attachment. Melt the chocolate at 50-55°C in the microwave or a bain-marie. In a saucepan, mix the sugar, cornflour and oat milk, add the deodorised coconut oil and bring to the boil. Pour over the melted chocolate in three batches. Whisk in the whipped potato protein mixture.

FOR THE DARK CHOCOLATE GLAZE
70 g dark chocolate (Hacienda Eleonor Pure Origin Ecuador 64% Valrhona® cocoa)
42 g still mineral water
12.9 g deodorised coconut oil
0.5 g xanthan gum
120 g neutral glaze

Melt the chocolate at 45-50°C in the microwave or a bain-marie. Heat the still mineral water to 45°C and pour over the melted deodorised coconut oil, followed by the xanthan gum. Using an immersion blender, blend for 1 minute until smooth. Reheat this mixture to 45°C and pour over the melted chocolate. Add the warmed neutral glaze. Blend to obtain a smooth glaze.
(Cont.)

FOR THE DARK CHOCOLATE PETALS
200 g dark chocolate (64% Valrhona® cocoa)

First, temper the chocolate to keep it shiny, smooth and stable. Chop the chocolate with a serrated knife and place in an earthenware bowl, then melt it in a bain-marie. Stir gently with a wooden spoon until it reaches 50-55°C. Remove the chocolate from the bain-marie. Place the bowl in a second bowl filled with water and 4-5 ice cubes. Stir the melted chocolate from time to time as it will start to set on the sides of the bowl. As soon as it reaches 27-28°C, return the bowl to the bain-marie, keeping a close eye on the temperature. When it reaches 31-32°C, the chocolate is tempered.

Place a board covered with a 40 x 4 cm plastic sheet on the work surface. Using a piping bag without a tip, pipe drops of chocolate previously melted in the microwave oven. Place a second 40 x 4 cm plastic sheet in contact with the chocolate, smoothing with your finger. Remove and place the two sheets of plastic with the chocolate petals in individual log or tuile moulds.

FOR FINISHING
Cornflowers (as needed)

ASSEMBLY AND FINISHING

Place a stainless steel ring 20 cm in diameter and 4 cm high on a baking tray lined with greaseproof paper. On the inside, line with a 4 cm high strip of plastic. Place the baked crumble disc on top and, using a piping bag without a tip, pipe a thin layer of dark chocolate mousse. Place the disc of chocolate biscuit, chocolate and blackcurrant ganache and blackcurrant compote on top, fill completely with mousse and smooth with an offset spatula. Leave to set in the fridge for 2 hours. Freeze for 5 hours before removing the ring and plastic band.

Place the frozen cake on a wire rack in a casserole dish. Using a ladle, coat the whole cake with the dark chocolate glaze and smooth the top with an offset spatula to remove any excess glaze. Place the dessert in a serving dish and leave to defrost in the fridge for 3 hours. Decorate with chocolate petals and dried cornflowers. Keep in the fridge until ready to use.

Rose des sables tart

This 'desert rose' tart was the link in our collaboration: chocolate for La Maison du Chocolat and the rose for me. A balance of rose, chocolate with notes of roasted almonds and almond praline, the flavours of which come together and then harmonise to create a unique taste, against a background of crisp pastry and silky ganache.

Pierre Hermé

Makes 10 individual tarts

Preparation time: 6 hours
Resting time: 12 hours
Cooking time: 20 minutes

HOMEMADE ALMOND PRALINE (PREPARE THE DAY BEFORE)
165 g caster sugar
50 g still mineral water
3 g (2 pieces) vanilla pods, used and dried
265 g blanched almonds

On a baking tray lined with greaseproof paper, spread out the almonds, taking care that they don't overlap. Bake in a fan oven at 160°C for 15 minutes. Cook the sugar and water in a saucepan until a thermometer or electronic probe reads 121°C. Pour the hot syrup over the crushed used vanilla pods and the warm blanched, roasted almonds. Mix and leave to caramelise over a medium heat. Remove to a non-stick baking tray to cool. Crush coarsely and grind in a food processor to a paste. Set aside in the fridge until ready to use. The praline will be used to fill the tart shells and to make the smooth cream.

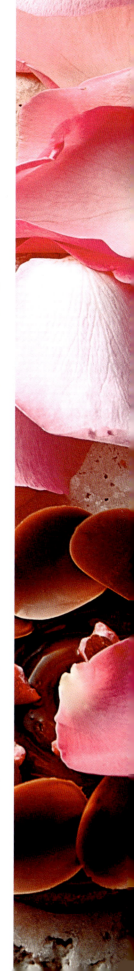

FOR THE SMOOTH ALMOND CREAM (PREPARE THE DAY BEFORE)

68 g still mineral water
6.7 g inverted sugar
17 g glucose syrup
14 g cocoa butter (Valrhona®)
88 g pure roasted almond butter
47 g homemade almond praline

Heat the still mineral water to 45°C, checking using a thermometer or electronic probe. Add the inverted sugar and glucose syrup and bring to the boil. Pour over the cocoa butter, pure almond butter and homemade almond praline in three batches, mixing each time, then blend with an immersion blender to obtain a smooth cream. Pour into a casserole dish, cover with cling film in direct contact and leave to cool in the fridge for around 12 hours before use.

FOR THE SWEET SHORTCRUST PASTRY

35 g deodorised coconut oil
35 g cocoa butter (Valrhona®)
80 g ground almonds
2 g Guérande fleur de sel
90 g icing sugar
75 g still mineral water
235 g flour

Melt the deodorised coconut oil and cocoa butter at 30-35°C, checking using a thermometer or electronic probe. Pour the ground almonds, fleur de sel and icing sugar into the bowl of a food processor fitted with a flat beater attachment, then add the coconut oil and cocoa butter mixture at 30°C. Blend until well incorporated, then add the still mineral water (heated to 40°C). Add the sifted flour. Place on a baking tray, cover with cling film in direct contact and refrigerate for 2 hours.

On a lightly floured work surface, roll out the pastry to a thickness of around 2-3 mm. Using rings, cut out 10 discs 12 cm in diameter. Place on a baking tray in the fridge for 30 minutes before baking. Grease 10 stainless steel rings 8 cm in diameter and 2 cm high, line them with the pastry and trim off any excess. Refrigerate for 1 hour before placing in the freezer for at least 2 hours. Preheat the fan oven to 250°C. Just before placing in the oven, lower the temperature to 170°C. Place the pastry shells on a baking tray lined with greaseproof paper, line with aluminium foil or greaseproof paper and fill with dried beans. Bake at 170°C for about 20 minutes. Remove from the oven and allow to cool, then remove the dried beans and foil. Keep the stainless steel rings for the rest of the assembly.

FOR THE ALMOND MILK CHOCOLATE AND ROSE GANACHE
136 g almond milk chocolate (Amatika 46% Valrhona® cocoa)
136 g oat milk
4 g natural rose flavouring

Chop the chocolate. Bring the oat milk to the boil in a saucepan, then pour over the chocolate. Stir starting from the centre and working outwards. Add the natural rose flavouring, then using an immersion blender, blend the ganache. Pour into a casserole dish, cover with cling film in direct contact and leave to cool in the fridge before use.

FOR THE ALMOND MILK CHOCOLATE PETALS
100 g almond milk chocolate (Amatika 46% Valrhona® cocoa)

Cut 20 plastic sheets 40 x 4 cm. On the work surface, place a board covered with a plastic sheet. Using a bag without a tip, pipe 10 drops of 0.5 g of almond milk chocolate, previously melted in the microwave. Place a second sheet of 40 x 4 cm plastic in contact with the chocolate and smooth out the drops with your finger. Place each layered sheet in individual log moulds.

ASSEMBLY AND FINISHING
Pink rose petals (as needed)
Glucose syrup (as needed)
Crushed pink pralines

Fill the pastry shells with homemade almond praline, then with almond milk chocolate and rose ganache, up to the top. Leave to set in the fridge for 30 minutes. Once the ganache has set, using a piping bag without a tip, pipe a spiral of smooth almond cream. Sprinkle with crushed pink pralines and place 9 almond milk chocolate petals around the edge of the tart. Decorate the top with a rose petal and a drop of glucose syrup dew. Keep in the fridge until ready to use.

Chocolate mousse

Chocolate mousse is a universal dessert that's as indulgent as you could wish for. This is my favourite recipe; it's so creamy and light.

Linda Vongdara

Serves 6-8

Preparation time: 1 hour
Resting time: 6 hours
Cooking time: 10 minutes

FOR THE CHOCOLATE SHARDS WITH FLEUR DE SEL
200 g dark chocolate (Satilia Noire 62% Valrhona® cocoa)
3.6 g Guérande fleur de sel

Finely crush the fleur de sel crystals with a rolling pin, then sieve through a medium/fine sieve. Set aside the finest crystals. First, temper the chocolate to keep it shiny, smooth and stable. Chop the chocolate with a serrated knife and place in an earthenware bowl, then melt it in a bain-marie. Stir gently with a wooden spoon until it reaches 50-55°C. Remove the chocolate from the bain-marie. Place the bowl in a second bowl filled with water and 4-5 ice cubes. Stir the melted chocolate from time to time as it will start to set on the sides of the bowl. As soon as it reaches 27-28°C, return the bowl to the bain-marie, keeping a close eye on the temperature. When it reaches 31-32°C, the chocolate is tempered. Stir in the crushed fleur de sel. On a plastic sheet, thinly spread the tempered fleur de sel chocolate to a thickness of about 1 cm. Place a second plastic sheet and a weight on top to prevent the chocolate from warping as it sets. Refrigerate for at least 1 hour. Coarsely break the fleur de sel chocolate slabs into 5-7 cm shards for decoration. Store in an airtight container in the fridge.

(Cont.)

FOR THE CHOCOLATE MOUSSE
400 g oat milk
125 g vanilla soya milk
15 g cornflour
300 g dark chocolate (Satilia Noire 62% Valrhona® cocoa)
180 g margarine
60 g liquid yumgo white (or 95 g aquafaba)
40 g light brown sugar
1 g Guérande fleur de sel

Bring the vegan milks and cornflour to the boil in a saucepan. Emulsify the hot mixture with an immersion blender, add the dark chocolate, blend, then add the margarine and blend again to obtain a ganache. Cool to 35°C. Whisk the yumgo white with the light brown sugar, adding the latter gradually. Gradually fold the yumgo and sugar mixture into the chocolate ganache and add the fleur de sel. Pour the mixture into the containers and leave to cool in the fridge. Just before serving, take a shard of fleur de sel chocolate and stick it into the chocolate mousse.

Chocolate praline bonbon with almonds, pumpkin seeds and za'atar

I came up with this chocolate bonbon on my return from a trip to Israel. The idea of using za'atar, a mixture of thyme, sesame and spices, to create a vegan recipe was clear to me.

Pierre Hermé

Makes 80 chocolate bonbons

Preparation time: 6 hours
Resting time: 12 hours
Cooking time: 20 minutes

FOR THE PUMPKIN SEED PRALINE WITH ZA'ATAR (PREPARE TWO DAYS BEFORE)
200 g pumpkin seeds
125 g caster sugar
37.5 g still mineral water
1.5 g Guérande fleur de sel
28 g grapeseed oil
8.5 g za'atar

On a baking tray lined with greaseproof paper, spread out the pumpkin seeds, taking care that they don't overlap. Place in a fan oven at 150°C for 10 minutes until the seeds are golden brown and crunchy. Cook the sugar and water in a saucepan until a thermometer or electronic probe reads 121°C. Pour the hot syrup over the warm roasted pumpkin seeds. Mix gently with a wooden spatula, then leave to caramelise over a medium heat. Transfer to a non-stick silicone mat to cool. Coarsely crush the caramelised pumpkin seeds and transfer to the bowl of a food processor. Add the fleur de sel, za'atar and grapeseed oil, and blend until you obtain a paste that should not be too finely ground. Set aside in the fridge.

Note: The caramelised pumpkin seeds must be crushed, ground and used as soon as they have cooled. Once they have been caramelised, they must not be stored as they can absorb moisture and this would alter the quality of the praline.

FOR THE ROASTED PUMPKIN SEEDS (PREPARE THE DAY BEFORE)
200 g pumpkin seeds

On a baking tray lined with greaseproof paper, spread out the pumpkin seeds, taking care that they don't overlap. Place in a fan oven at 150°C for 10 minutes until the seeds are golden brown and crunchy. They will be needed to make the praline and decorate the chocolate bonbons.

FOR THE ALMOND, PUMPKIN SEED AND ZA'ATAR PRALINE (PREPARE TWO DAYS BEFORE)
170 g almond praline (60% almonds)
400 g pumpkin seed and za'atar praline
75 g dark chocolate (Araguani 72% Valrhona® cocoa)
112 g cocoa butter (Valrhona®)
80 g roasted pumpkin seeds

Add the almond praline and pumpkin seed and za'atar praline to the bowl of a food processor, along with the melted dark chocolate and cocoa butter. Mix until it reaches 24°C, checking using a thermometer or electronic probe. Quickly add the roasted pumpkin seeds and mix. Make sure the temperature does not exceed 25°C. Prepare a plastic sheet and a 30 x 30 cm, 12 mm thick baking frame on a baking tray. Pour in the praline and spread evenly with an offset spatula. Leave to cool at room temperature (in a room at 16-18°C) overnight.

FOR CUTTING OUT THE PRALINES (PREPARE THE DAY BEFORE)
250 g dark chocolate (Araguani 72% Valrhona® cocoa)

The next day, prepare the pre-coating for the pralines. First, temper the dark chocolate to keep it shiny, smooth and stable. Chop the chocolate with a serrated knife and place in an earthenware bowl, then melt it in a bain-marie. Stir gently with a wooden spoon until it reaches 50-55°C. Remove the chocolate from the bain-marie. Place the bowl in a second bowl filled with water and 4-5 ice cubes. Stir the melted chocolate from time to time as it will start to set on the sides of the bowl. As soon as it reaches 27-28°C, return the bowl to the bain-marie, keeping a close eye on the temperature. When it reaches 31-32°C, the chocolate is tempered.
Spread the tempered chocolate in a thin layer over

the almond, pumpkin seed and za'atar praline you prepared the day before. Smooth with a palette knife and leave to set for 20 minutes at room temperature. Turn the frame over onto the plastic sheet and spread a thin layer of dark chocolate over the underside of the praline. Smooth and leave to set for 20 minutes at room temperature.

Then remove the frame by sliding a small knife blade dipped in hot water around it. Cut out 30 x 22.5 mm rectangles and remove. Place them on a baking tray, spacing them out. Store at room temperature (16-18°C) overnight.

FOR THE FINAL CHOCOLATE BONBONS COATING
500 g dark chocolate (Araguani 72% Valrhona® cocoa)

Now carry out the final coating of the chocolate bonbons. First, temper the chocolate as described above; it should be 31-32°C. Prepare several plastic sheets on which to place the chocolate bonbons.

Dip the first praline rectangle into the tempered chocolate. Then remove it with a three-pronged chocolate fork. On one side of the bowl, gradually moving the fork towards you, place the praline back into the chocolate, pushing the fork in and then lifting it, two or three times, so that the praline is coated in the chocolate. Remove the fork with the bonbon; tap it to remove the excess chocolate then scrape it over the edge of the bowl. Place the bonbon on a plastic sheet and place three whole roasted pumpkin seeds on top.

Repeat the process for the other pralines, taking care to place the bowl of chocolate in a bain-marie from time to time so that the temperature remains 31-32°C. Leave the bonbons to dry at room temperature overnight.

Store the chocolate bonbons in an airtight container at 15-18°C, away from odours and humidity.

'The coating should be thin, but not ultra-thin, as is the current trend among our colleagues. The coating contributes to the taste and balance of a chocolate bonbon and must be present without dominating.'

Pierre Hermé

Almond praline and curry chocolate bonbon

I've made an almond praline with a hint of vanilla. As an invitation to travel, I've added Bombay curry, which I particularly like for its balance of fresh notes and warm flavours. I chose a coating that was thin enough but not too thin, as the thickness of the chocolate also contributes to the emotions involved in eating it.

Pierre Hermé

Makes 80 chocolate bonbons

Preparation time: 6 hours
Resting time: 12 hours
Cooking time: 15 minutes

HOMEMADE ALMOND AND VANILLA PRALINE (PREPARE THE DAY BEFORE)
200 g whole white almonds
125 g caster sugar
37.5 g still mineral water
1½ Madagascar vanilla pods, split and scraped

On a baking tray lined with greaseproof paper, spread out the almonds, taking care that they don't overlap. Bake in a fan oven at 160°C for 15 minutes. Cook the sugar and water in a saucepan until a thermometer or electronic probe reads 121°C. Pour the hot syrup over the split and scraped vanilla pods and the warm roasted almonds. Mix gently with a wooden spatula, then leave to caramelise over a medium heat. Transfer to a non-stick silicone mat to cool. Coarsely crush the caramelised almonds and place them in the bowl of a food processor. Mix to obtain a paste that should not be too finely ground. Set aside in the fridge.

Note: caramelised almonds must be crushed, ground and used as soon as they have cooled. Once they have been caramelised, they must not be stored as they can absorb moisture and this would alter the quality of the praline.

FOR THE ALMOND AND CURRY PRALINE (PREPARE THE DAY BEFORE)

60 g dark chocolate (Araguani 72% Valrhona® cocoa)
90 g cocoa butter (Valrhona®)
330 g almond praline (60% almonds)
330 g homemade almond and vanilla praline
1.25 g Guérande fleur de sel
4.5 g Bombay curry (Rœllinger®)

Temper the dark chocolate and cocoa butter together. Chop the chocolate and cocoa butter with a serrated knife and place in an earthenware bowl, then melt over a bain-marie. Stir gently with a wooden spoon until the mixture reaches 45-50°C. Remove the chocolate/cocoa butter mixture from the bain-marie. Place the bowl in a second bowl filled with water and 4-5 ice cubes. Stir the mixture from time to time as it will start to set on the sides of the bowl. As soon as the chocolate/cocoa butter mixture reaches 27-28°C, return the bowl to the bain-marie, keeping a close eye on the temperature. When it reaches 31-32°C, the chocolate is tempered.

Stir in the remaining ingredients and use immediately. Place a plastic sheet and a 30 x 30 cm, 12 mm thick baking frame on a baking tray. Pour in the praline and spread evenly with an offset spatula. Leave to cool at room temperature (at 16-18°C) overnight.

FOR CUTTING OUT THE PRALINES (PREPARE THE DAY BEFORE)

250 g almond milk chocolate (Amatika 46% Valrhona® cocoa)

Prepare the pre-coating for the pralines.

First, temper the chocolate to keep it shiny, smooth and stable. Chop the chocolate with a serrated knife and place in an earthenware bowl, then melt it in a bain-marie. Stir gently with a wooden spoon until it reaches 45-50°C. Remove the chocolate from the bain-marie. Place the bowl in a second bowl filled with water and 4-5 ice cubes. Stir the melted chocolate from time to time as it will start to set on the sides of the bowl. As soon as it reaches 27-28°C, return the bowl to the bain-marie, keeping a close eye on the temperature. When it reaches 30-31°C, the chocolate is tempered.

Spread the chocolate in a thin layer over the praline you prepared the day before. Smooth with an offset spatula and leave to set for 20 minutes at room temperature. Turn the frame over onto the plastic sheet and spread a thin layer of chocolate over the underside of the praline. Smooth and leave to set for 20 minutes at room temperature.

Then remove the frame by sliding a small knife blade dipped in hot water around it. Cut out 30 x 22.5 mm rectangles and remove. Place them on a baking tray, spacing them out. Store at room temperature (16-18°C) overnight.

FOR THE FINAL CHOCOLATE BONBONS COATING
500 g dark chocolate (Ampamakia 64% Valrhona® cocoa)
Whole roasted blanched almonds (as needed)

Now carry out the final coating of the chocolate bonbons. First, temper the chocolate as described above; it should be 30-31°C. Prepare several plastic sheets on which to place the chocolate bonbons.

Dip the first praline rectangle into the tempered chocolate. Then remove it with a three-pronged chocolate fork. On one side of the bowl, gradually moving the fork towards you, place the praline back into the chocolate, pushing the fork in and then lifting it, two or three times, so that the praline is coated in the chocolate. Remove the fork with the bonbon; tap it to remove the excess chocolate then scrape it over the edge of the bowl. Place the bonbon on a plastic sheet and place a whole roasted almond diagonally across the top. Repeat the process for the other pralines, taking care to place the bowl of chocolate in a bain-marie from time to time so that the temperature remains 30-31°C.

Leave the bonbons to dry at room temperature overnight. Store the chocolate bonbons in an airtight container at 15-18°C, away from odours and humidity.

'The coating should be thin, but not ultra-thin, as is the current trend among our colleagues. The coating contributes to the taste and balance of a chocolate bonbon and must be present without dominating.'

Pierre Hermé

Chocolate truffles

Melt-in-the-mouth, rich and intense, truffles are timeless treats that highlight the flavours of chocolate.

Linda Vongdara

Makes 50 truffles

Preparation time: 30 minutes
Resting time: 2 hours minimum
Cooking time: 10 minutes

FOR THE CHOCOLATE TRUFFLES
110 g dark chocolate (Araguani 72% Valrhona® cocoa)
110 g dark chocolate (64% Valrhona® cocoa)
50 g oat milk
60 g soya milk
30 g light brown sugar
70 g white almond butter
95 g deodorised coconut oil
1 g Guérande fleur de sel
100 g cocoa powder

Chop the chocolates. In a saucepan, whisk together the soya milk, oat milk and light brown sugar. Bring the mixture to the boil over a medium heat. Pour the liquid over the chopped chocolates, leave to melt for a few moments then blend with an immersion blender to emulsify the ganache. Add the almond butter, deodorised coconut oil and fleur de sel and blend again. The mixture should be smooth, shiny and homogeneous. Pour the ganache into a 15 cm square baking frame and leave to cool. Leave in the fridge for at least 2 hours to harden. Once solidified, cut out rectangles measuring approximately 3 x 2 cm and cover with cocoa powder. Store the truffles in an airtight container in the fridge and serve chilled.

Fruit desserts and tarts

Fruity and sweet

You'd think that fruit desserts would be easier to make because the fruit predominates, but that's not the case. The recipes must be prepared with the same precision and attention to detail, in order to elevate the flavours and aromas of each fruit, in the absence of animal fats.

What's more, most vegan ingredients have a more discreet flavour than their animal-based counterparts, leaving more room for the expression of taste. This must be taken into account to find the right balance.

My main challenge here was to recreate Fetish Ispahan and Jardin de l'Atlas in vegan versions, using the classic versions as a reference point. These creations offer a different interpretation of gourmandise. For the Ispahan, the vegan meringue was our first challenge. We had to find the texture we love in macarons: both crunchy and soft. And I have to admit that it's extremely gratifying to be able to reproduce such pleasant sensations in these creations, where it's very hard to tell the difference.

In the same way, for the babas, the results obtained with the dough surprised and even amazed me. The texture is slightly different, but retains the moist feel that makes babas so special; the freshness is also accentuated. Of course, when it comes to creams, we had to learn how to handle coconut oil, xanthan gum and, above all, liquid lecithin, which can have an unpleasant taste if not used in the right quantities.

We've also developed a vegan pastry dough and have come up with three new recipes. The use of vegetable oils and flour blends brings out the flavour of the main ingredient, which, freed from the taste of butter, reveals different, often more pronounced facets. The Infinitely yuzu tart reveals a citrus flavour that is difficult to achieve in a traditional cake, where dairy products and eggs temper the liveliness of the fruit. The Pecan pie – inspired by one of my creations, the Odyssey – is also incredibly distinctive in flavour. The chosen non-dairy cream allows the pecans to express themselves fully, while the walnut liqueur and Okinawa black sugar with their liquorice notes underline the aromas.

For each of these creations, the taste comes first, and the work with textures brings out the deliciousness.

Enchanted garden tart

I first imagined this combination in a macaron. Then I had the idea of using it in a tart. I particularly like the contrast between the freshness of the lime non-dairy cream and the heat of the Espelette pepper, then the punch provided by the liveliness of the fresh raspberries topped with a lime jelly.

Pierre Hermé

Makes 10 individual tarts

Preparation time: 6 hours
Resting time: 6 hours
Cooking time: 40 minutes

FOR THE SWEET SHORTCRUST PASTRY
35 g deodorised coconut oil
35 g cocoa butter (Valrhona®)
80 g ground almonds
2 g Guérande fleur de sel
90 g icing sugar
75 g still mineral water
235 g flour

Melt the deodorised coconut oil and cocoa butter at 30-35°C, checking using a thermometer or electronic probe. Pour the ground almonds, fleur de sel and icing sugar into the bowl of a food processor fitted with a flat beater attachment, then add the melted coconut oil and cocoa butter mixture at 30°C. Blend until well incorporated, then add the still mineral water (heated to 40°C). Add the sifted flour. Place on a baking tray, cover with cling film in direct contact and refrigerate for 2 hours.

On a lightly floured work surface, roll out the pastry to a thickness of around 2-3 mm. Using rings, cut out 10 discs 12 cm in diameter. Place on a baking tray in the fridge for 30 minutes before baking. Grease 10 stainless steel rings 8 cm in diameter and 2 cm high, line them with the pastry and trim off any excess. Refrigerate for 1 hour before placing in the freezer for at least 2 hours.

Preheat the fan oven to 250°C. Just before placing in the oven, lower the temperature to 170°C. Place the pastry shells on a baking tray lined with greaseproof paper, line with aluminium foil or greaseproof paper and fill with dried beans. Bake at 170°C for about 20 minutes. Remove from the oven and allow to cool, then remove the dried beans and foil. Keep the stainless steel rings for the rest of the assembly.

FOR THE GLUTEN-FREE FLOUR MIX
50 g semi-wholegrain rice flour
30 g cornflour
10 g potato starch
10 g ground almonds

Sift all the ingredients together and use immediately.

FOR THE ALMOND CREAM WITH LIME AND ESPELETTE PEPPER
10 g potato starch
50 g lime juice
100 g still mineral water
60 g deodorised coconut oil
135 g ground almonds
5 g citrus fibre
135 g icing sugar
0.5 g Guérande fleur de sel
55 g gluten-free flour mix
2.5 g lime zest
4.5 g Espelette pepper
25 g grapeseed or rapeseed oil

In a saucepan, mix together the potato starch with the lime juice and still mineral water, then bring to the boil. Place in a casserole dish, cover with cling film in direct contact and set aside in the fridge. Melt the deodorised coconut oil at 30-35°C, checking using a thermometer or electronic probe. Add the ground almonds, citrus fibre, icing sugar, fleur de sel, gluten-free flour mix, lime zest and Espelette pepper to the bowl of a food processor fitted with a flat beater attachment, then add the oils. Mix and stir in the potato starch/water/juice mixture. Use immediately.

COOKING

Top the tart shells with 18 g of almond cream and bake in a fan oven at 170°C for around 15 minutes. Remove from the oven, leave to cool and set aside for assembly.

FOR THE LIME JELLY
30 g caster sugar
3.5 g agar-agar powder
170 g lime juice

In a mixing bowl, combine the sugar and agar-agar powder. In a saucepan, heat the lime juice to 40°C, checking using a thermometer or electronic probe, then sprinkle in the sugar/agar-agar mixture. Bring the mixture to the boil, stirring regularly with a spatula. Place in a casserole dish, cover with cling film in direct contact and leave to cool completely in the fridge. Before use, blend the mixture in a food processor to transform it into a smooth, supple gel.

ASSEMBLY AND FINISHING
500 g fresh raspberries
2 limes

Place the raspberries on top of the cooked and cooled almond cream tart shells, which have previously been brushed with lime jelly. Using a piping bag, fill the gaps with lime jelly. Using a Microplane® grater, grate the lime zest over the tarts. Keep in the fridge until ready to use.

Note: the Espelette pepper must be from the current year, to make sure it is fragrant and flavoursome.

Infinitely yuzu tart

The advantage of vegan ingredients is undoubtedly their fairly neutral taste. Without butter or cream, the fruit has a freer and more intense flavour. This tart is an example of this, with all the facets of yuzu: fragrant, powerful and intense.

Pierre Hermé

Makes 10 individual tarts

Preparation time: 6 hours
Resting time: 13 hours
Cooking time: 30 minutes

FOR THE YUZU CREAM (PREPARE THE DAY BEFORE)
4 g organic lemon zest
100 g caster sugar
3.5 g pectin NH
2.5 g citrus fibre
10 g cornflour
75 g still mineral water
225 g Kôchi yuzu juice
50 g cocoa butter (Valrhona®)
50 g deodorised coconut oil

Using a Microplane® grater, grate the lemon zest. Mix the sugar, zest, pectin, citrus fibre and cornflour. Heat the mineral water and yuzu juice in a saucepan to 40°C, using a thermometer or electronic probe to check the temperature, then sprinkle in the previous mixture. Bring to the boil and pour over the cocoa butter and deodorised coconut oil. Using an immersion blender, blend for several minutes to emulsify. Place in a casserole dish, cover with cling film in direct contact and leave to cool and set in the fridge for around 12 hours.

FRUIT DESSERTS AND TARTS *Fruity and sweet*

FOR THE SWEET SHORTCRUST PASTRY

35 g deodorised coconut oil
35 g cocoa butter (Valrhona®)
80 g ground almonds
2 g Guérande fleur de sel
90 g icing sugar
75 g still mineral water
235 g flour

Melt the deodorised coconut oil and cocoa butter at 30-35°C, checking using a thermometer or electronic probe. Pour the ground almonds, fleur de sel and icing sugar into the bowl of a food processor fitted with a flat beater attachment, then add the oil/cocoa butter mixture at 30°C. Blend until well incorporated, then add the still mineral water (heated to 40°C). Add the sifted flour. Place on a baking tray, cover with cling film in direct contact and refrigerate for 2 hours.

On a lightly floured work surface, roll out the pastry to a thickness of around 2-3 mm. Using rings, cut out 10 discs 12 cm in diameter. Place on a baking tray in the fridge for 30 minutes before baking. Grease 10 stainless steel rings 8 cm in diameter and 2 cm high, line them with the pastry and trim off any excess. Refrigerate for 1 hour before placing in the freezer for at least 2 hours. Preheat the fan oven to 250°C. Just before placing in the oven, lower the temperature to 170°C. Place the pastry shells on a baking tray lined with greaseproof paper, line the shells with aluminium foil or greaseproof paper and fill with dried beans. Bake at 170°C for about 20 minutes. Remove from the oven and allow to cool, then remove the dried beans and foil. Keep the stainless steel rings for the rest of the assembly.

FOR THE GLUTEN-FREE FLOUR MIX

50 g semi-wholegrain rice flour
30 g cornflour
10 g potato starch
10 g ground almonds

Sift all the ingredients together and use immediately.

FOR THE YUZU ALMOND CREAM

4 g potato starch
36 g Kôchi yuzu juice
24 g still mineral water
24 g deodorised coconut oil
55 g ground almonds
2 g citrus fibre
55 g icing sugar
21 g gluten-free flour mix
10 g grapeseed or rapeseed oil

In a saucepan, mix the potato starch with the yuzu juice and still mineral water, then bring to the boil. Place in a casserole dish, cover with cling film in direct contact and set aside in the fridge. Melt the deodorised coconut oil at 30-35°C, checking using a thermometer or electronic probe. Add the ground almonds, citrus fibre, sugar and gluten-free flour mix to the bowl of a food processor fitted with a flat beater attachment, then add the oils. Mix and then add the potato starch/water/yuzu juice mixture. Use immediately.

COOKING

Top the cooked pastry shells with 18 g of yuzu almond cream and bake in a fan oven at 170°C for around 10 minutes. Remove from the oven, leave to cool and set aside for assembly.

FOR THE HOMEMADE KÔCHI YUZU PURÉE

5 g caster sugar
5 g pectin NH
65 g Kôchi yuzu juice
125 g candied yuzu peel
25 g still mineral water

Mix together the sugar and pectin. Using a food processor, blend the juice and candied yuzu peel into small pieces. In a saucepan, heat the water and peel/juice mixture to 40°C, checking using a thermometer or electronic probe. Sprinkle in the sugar and pectin. Bring to the boil. Set aside in the fridge.

ASSEMBLY AND FINISHING

Neutral glaze (as needed)

Spread 7 g of Kôchi yuzu purée over the cooked almond cream tart shells, then use a piping bag without a tip to top with the yuzu cream. Using a palette knife, smooth the cream flush with the top of the tart shell and place in the freezer for a few minutes. When the cream has set, using a small palette knife, smooth the Kôchi yuzu purée over one side of the tart. Refrigerate for 1 hour. Melt the neutral glaze in the microwave or over a low heat. Dip the tarts into the hot glaze and brush off any excess. Keep in the fridge until ready to use.

Infinitely pecan pie

For this pie, I play with the flavours of pecan and Okinawa black sugar and highlight them with touch of walnut liqueur. An infinitely delicious, multi-textured tart.

Pierre Hermé

Makes 2 tarts for 6-8 people

Preparation time: 6 hours
Resting time: 6 hours
Cooking time: 1 hour

FOR THE SWEET SHORTCRUST PASTRY

35 g deodorised coconut oil
35 g cocoa butter (Valrhona®)
80 g ground almonds
2 g Guérande fleur de sel
90 g icing sugar
75 g still mineral water
235 g flour

Melt the deodorised coconut oil and cocoa butter at 30-35°C, checking using a thermometer or electronic probe. Pour the ground almonds, fleur de sel and icing sugar into the bowl of a food processor fitted with a flat beater attachment, then add the coconut oil and cocoa butter mixture at 30°C. Blend until well incorporated, then add the still mineral water (heated to 40°C). Add the sifted flour. Place on a baking tray, cover with cling film in direct contact and refrigerate for 2 hours.

On a lightly floured work surface, roll out the pastry to a thickness of around 2-3 mm. Using rings, cut out 10 discs 12 cm in diameter. Place on a baking tray in the fridge for 30 minutes before baking. Grease 10 stainless steel rings 8 cm in diameter and 2 cm high, line them with the pastry and trim off any excess. Refrigerate for 1 hour before placing in the freezer for at least 2 hours. Preheat the fan oven to 250°C. Just before placing in the oven, lower the temperature to 170°C. Place the pastry shells on a baking tray lined with greaseproof paper, line the shells with aluminium foil or greaseproof paper and fill with dried beans. Bake at 170°C for about 20 minutes. Remove from the oven and allow to cool, then remove the beans and foil. Keep the stainless steel rings for the rest of the assembly.

FRUIT DESSERTS AND TARTS *Fruity and sweet*

FOR THE HOMEMADE PECAN PRALINE

150 g pecans
100 g caster sugar
2 g vanilla powder

On a baking tray lined with greaseproof paper, spread out the pecan nuts, taking care that they don't overlap. Bake in a fan oven at 150°C for 5 minutes. In a saucepan, caramelise the sugar with the vanilla powder at 175°C, checking using a thermometer or electronic probe. Add the pecans to the caramel and mix well. Transfer to a non-stick silicone mat to cool. Coarsely crush the caramelised pecans and place them in the bowl of a food processor. Mix to obtain a paste that should not be too finely ground. Use immediately or keep refrigerated.

Note: the caramelised pecans must be crushed, ground and used as soon as they have cooled. Once they have been caramelised, they must not be stored as they can absorb moisture and this would alter the quality of the praline.

FOR THE OKINAWA BLACK SUGAR PECAN PIE SHELL

3.75 g cornflour
0.5 g agar-agar powder
7.5 g rice cream
225 g oat milk
150 g Okinawa black sugar
40 g deodorised coconut oil
50 g homemade pecan praline
0.6 g Guérande fleur de sel
285 g chopped pecan nuts

Sift together the cornflour, agar-agar and rice cream. Bring the oat milk and 50 g of the black sugar to the boil in a saucepan. Mix the cornflour/agar-agar/rice cream mixture with the remaining 100 g of black sugar. Mix this mixture with half the oat milk/black sugar mixture before adding the other half. Bring the rice cream, cornflour and agar-agar mixture to the boil, stirring briskly with a whisk. Remove from the heat and add the deodorised coconut oil, praline, fleur de sel and chopped pecans. Place the mixture in a casserole dish, cover with cling film in direct contact and leave to cool in the fridge.

Note: the rice cream comes in powder form.

FOR THE PECAN NUT CHANTILLY CREAM

3.75 g cornflour
0.5 g agar-agar powder
7.5 g rice cream
95 g oat milk
63 g Okinawa black sugar
17 g deodorised coconut oil
21 g homemade pecan praline
0.6 g Guérande fleur de sel

Sift together the cornflour, agar-agar and rice cream. Bring the oat milk and 20 g of the black sugar to the boil in a saucepan. Mix the cornflour/agar-agar/rice cream mixture with the remaining 43 g of black sugar. Mix this mixture with half the oat milk/black sugar mixture before adding the other half. Bring the mixture to the boil, stirring briskly with a whisk. Remove from the heat and add the deodorised coconut oil, praline and fleur de sel. Place the mixture in a casserole dish, cover with cling film in direct contact and leave to cool in the fridge.

FOR THE PECAN NUT AND WALNUT LIQUEUR CHANTILLY CREAM

600 g non-dairy cream (31% fat)
200 g pecan nut chantilly cream mixture
50 g walnut liqueur

In the bowl of a food processor fitted with a whisk attachment, whip the non-dairy cream. Gently fold in the chantilly cream mixture and the walnut liqueur using a spatula. Use immediately.

FOR THE PECAN NUT NOUGATINE

35 g still mineral water
35 g glucose syrup
100 g caster sugar
1.7 g pectin NH
45 g rapeseed or grapeseed oil
1.7 g citrus fibre
100 g chopped pecan nuts
1 pinch Guérande fleur de sel

In a saucepan, heat the water and glucose syrup to 45-50°C, checking using a thermometer or electronic probe. Add the sugar and pectin NH and heat to 106°C, checking using a thermometer or electronic probe. Add the oil and citrus fibre and blend using an immersion blender. Add the chopped pecans and fleur de sel. Pour onto a sheet of greaseproof paper, spread with a palette knife, cover with a second sheet of greaseproof paper and continue to spread using a rolling pin. Wrap in cling film and freeze for at least 2 hours. Cut the still-frozen sheets in half and place each half on a baking tray lined with a non-stick silicone mat. Cook in a fan oven at 170°C for 18-20 minutes. Remove from the oven, leave to cool for a few moments, then, using tin biscuit cutters, cut out two discs 17 cm in diameter. Use immediately or store in an airtight container at room temperature.

(Cont.)

FOR THE CARAMELISED PECAN NUTS
140 g pecans
500 g caster sugar
150 g still mineral water

On a baking tray lined with greaseproof paper, spread out the pecans, taking care that they don't overlap. Roast them in a fan oven at 150°C for 5 minutes. In a saucepan, heat the water and sugar to 118°C, checking using a thermometer or electronic probe, then add the warm pecans. Caramelise over a low heat while stirring with a wooden spatula. Pour the caramelised pecans onto a baking tray lined with a non-stick silicone mat, separate and leave to cool. Store in an airtight container.

ASSEMBLY AND FINISHING

Fill the two cooked pastry shells with 370 g Okinawa black sugar pecan pie filling. Bake in a fan oven at 160°C for around 30 minutes. Remove from the oven, leave to cool to room temperature and remove the rings. Using a piping bag fitted with an 8 cm diameter biscuit cutter, pipe 350 g of the pecan and walnut liqueur chantilly cream into each cooked tart shell. Place a disc of pecan nougatine and caramelised pecans on top. Keep in the fridge until ready to use.

Note: the Okinawa black sugar pecan pie pastry is very 'moist' so at the start of cooking it bubbles then it gradually dries out.

Passion fruit and mango dessert

For this dessert, fresh mango is accompanied by a fruit mousse with exotic flavours that are both rich and tangy.

Linda Vongdara

Serves 6-8

Preparation time: 6 hours
Resting time: 6 hours
Cooking time: 20-22 minutes

FOR THE SOFT GLUTEN-FREE BISCUIT
- 120 g light brown sugar
- 120 g sweetened plain soya milk (if unsweetened, add 12 g sugar per 100 g soya milk)
- 3 g cider vinegar
- 15 g oat flour or rolled oats, blended to a powder
- 105 g semi-wholegrain rice flour
- 15 g chickpea flour
- 45 g potato starch
- 7 g baking powder
- 45 g ground almonds
- 1 g xanthan gum
- 60 g deodorised coconut oil
- 60 g peanut or grapeseed oil

In the bowl of a food processor fitted with a flat beater attachment, blend the light brown sugar, soya milk and cider vinegar until the sugar has completely dissolved to increase the liquid mass. Add the oat/rice/chickpea flours together with the potato starch, baking powder, ground almonds and xanthan gum and mix well. Leave the starches to hydrate for about 20 minutes. Emulsify the mixture with the oils poured in gradually, at high speed. Pour the mixture onto a baking tray covered with greaseproof paper in a 40 x 30 cm stainless steel frame. Smooth the surface with an offset spatula and bake in a fan oven at 200°C for 10-12 minutes until golden brown. After cooking, leave to cool and cover with cling film in direct contact until completely cool. Using a stainless steel ring, cut out a disc 14 cm in diameter. Crumble the remaining biscuit and put it back in a fan oven at 180°C for 10 minutes to dry and roast. It will be used to make the crispy base.

FOR THE CRISPY BASE
100 g Almond Inspiration (Valrhona®)
110 g soft gluten-free roasted biscuit
50 g ground almonds
1.5 g Guérande fleur de sel

Melt the Almond Inspiration in the microwave, then mix all the ingredients. Spread the mixture 5 mm thick between two sheets of greaseproof paper and place on a baking tray. Cool slightly in the fridge, then cut out a 14 cm diameter disc.

FOR THE MANGO AND PASSION FRUIT COMPOTE
200 g passion fruit purée
60 g light brown sugar
6 g pectin NH
200 g finely diced mango

Bring the passion fruit purée to the boil in a saucepan. Add the light brown sugar and pectin. Allow the pectin to dissolve while stirring for about 1 minute at a gentle simmer. Remove from the heat, add the diced mango and mix well. Pour into a 14 cm diameter ring, place the soft biscuit disc on top, leave to cool and place in the freezer before use.

FOR THE PASSION FRUIT AND MANGO MOUSSE
140 g coconut milk
70 g mango purée
80 g passion fruit purée
0.5 g agar-agar powder
25 g cocoa butter (Valrhona®)
95 g white raw almond butter
40 g liquid yumgo white (or 65 g aquafaba)
40 g light brown sugar

Bring the coconut milk, the two fruit purées and the agar-agar to the boil in a saucepan. Mix the hot mixture with the cocoa butter and almond butter using an immersion blender. Cool to 35°C. Whisk the yumgo with the light brown sugar, adding the latter gradually.

Gradually fold the yumgo and sugar mixture into the fruit mixture. Set aside in the fridge.

FOR THE MANGO ICING
90 g light brown sugar
24 g glucose syrup
4 g pectin NH
350 g mango purée

Bring the mango purée, 70 g of sugar and the glucose syrup to the boil in a saucepan. Add the remaining 20 g of sugar and pectin mixed together. Allow the pectin to dissolve while stirring for 1 minute at a gentle simmer. Leave to cool.

(Cont.)

ASSEMBLY

Place a stainless steel ring or mould 15 cm in diameter and 4 cm high on a baking tray lined with greaseproof paper. Pour the passion fruit and mango mousse a third of the way up, and place the frozen compote disc and soft biscuit disc on top. Pour more mousse almost flush with the mould and place the crispy base disc on top. Leave to cool for 1 hour in the fridge, then freeze for 4 hours.

FOR FINISHING
1 fresh mango, peeled and cut into 3 mm thick strips
1 passion fruit
100 g neutral glaze

Melt the mango icing at 50°C, then use it at 37°C. Turn out the dessert and place it on a stainless steel rack, placed on a plate or in a container. Pour the mango glaze over the dessert and allow any excess to drain off. Leave to set. Place the dessert on a serving dish and arrange the long thin strips of mango on top. Add a few dots of melted neutral glaze and sprinkle with passion fruit seeds. Refrigerate until ready to use.

FRUIT DESSERTS AND TARTS *Fruity and sweet*

Raspberry dessert

Picking raspberries is a summer treat that I never tire of. In this dessert, the fruit combines with the deep notes of muscovado sugar. The scents of the lime zest enhance the liveliness of the raspberry.

Linda Vongdara

Makes 10 individual cakes

Preparation time: 3 hours
Resting time: 7 hours
Cooking time: 50 minutes

FOR THE ALMOND AND MUSCOVADO SUGAR FONDANT BISCUIT
(1st LAYER OF LEONARD BISCUIT)

25 g deodorised coconut oil
25 g grapeseed oil
72 g soya milk
50 g muscovado sugar
60 g T45 fine wheat flour
15 g cornflour
5 g baking powder
30 g ground almonds
4 g ground chia seeds

Mix the melted deodorised coconut oil with the grapeseed oil to prevent the coconut oil from solidifying. Set aside at room temperature.

In the bowl of a food processor fitted with a flat beater attachment, blend the soya milk and sugar until completely dissolved to increase the liquid mass. Add the flour, cornflour, baking powder, ground almonds and ground chia seeds all at once, and mix until smooth. Leave the mixture for at least 20 minutes. After resting, emulsify the mixture at medium speed, adding the oils gradually, until the paste is smooth. Pour the mixture onto a 40 x 30 cm baking tray lined with a non-stick silicone mat. Spread out thinly and smooth the surface with an offset spatula. Freeze the biscuit dough to harden.

FOR THE ALMOND FONDANT
(2ND LAYER OF LEONARD BISCUIT)
85 g soya milk
47 g muscovado sugar
7 g potato starch
20 g grapeseed oil
50 g ground almonds

In a saucepan, mix the soya milk, muscovado sugar and potato starch. Place over a low heat to thicken. Remove from the heat and add the grapeseed oil and ground almonds. Whisk together. Leave to cool and spread the mixture over the first layer of frozen biscuit dough. Bake in a preheated fan oven at 180°C for around 12 minutes until golden brown on the surface. When cooked, leave to cool and cut into 10 discs 5 cm in diameter.

FOR THE RASPBERRY GEL WITH LIME ZEST
40 g caster sugar
3 g pectin NH
200 g raspberry purée
5 g organic lime zest

Take 20 g of sugar and mix with the pectin. Bring the raspberry purée and the remaining 20 g of sugar to the boil in a small saucepan. Add the sugar/pectin mixture and keep simmering over a low heat for a moment, until the pectin has completely dissolved. Add the lime zest, stir and leave the gel to cool completely. Transfer the mixture to a piping bag without a tip.

FOR THE RASPBERRY CRÉMEUX
276 g raspberry purée
84 g caster sugar
30 g rice cream
1.4 g agar-agar powder
180 g margarine

In a small saucepan, combine the raspberry purée, sugar, rice cream and agar-agar and bring to the boil. Remove from the heat, add the margarine and blend with an immersion blender. Use immediately.

FOR THE SWEET SHORTCRUST PASTRY
30 g cocoa butter (Valrhona®)
12 g grapeseed oil
90 g plain flour
25 g potato starch
40 g icing sugar
15 g ground almonds
42 g soya milk
2 g Guérande fleur de sel
Cocoa butter powder (as needed)

Mix the melted cocoa butter with the grapeseed oil. Set aside at room temperature. Mix the flour and potato starch with the grapeseed oil and cocoa butter mixture in the bowl of a food processor fitted with a flat beater attachment. Add the icing sugar and ground almonds and mix again. Pour in the soya milk and stop processing as the dough comes together. Sprinkle in the fleur de sel and knead the pastry by hand. Cover the pastry with cling film and place in the fridge for at least 20 minutes. Roll out the pastry to a thickness of 2 mm and cut into 6 cm diameter discs using a biscuit cutter. Bake the pastry in a fan oven at 170°C for 15 minutes, between two non-stick silicone mats. Sprinkle with cocoa butter when it comes out of the oven. Leave to cool.

FOR THE RASPBERRY FOMICO MOUSSE

45 g liquid yumgo white
40 g caster sugar
200 g raspberry purée
2 g agar-agar powder

In the bowl of a food processor fitted with a whisk attachment, whip the yumgo white and gradually add the sugar until the mixture is stiff. Bring the raspberry purée and agar-agar to the boil. Off the heat, add a third of the sweetened whipped yumgo to the pan and whisk quickly, then add the remaining two thirds and pour the hot mousse into the bowl of a food processor fitted with a whisk attachment. Finish by whisking quickly, from top to bottom. Using a tablespoon dipped in hot water, make quenelles of the mousse and place on a tray covered with cling film. Leave to set in the fridge.

FOR THE GLOSSY RASPBERRY ICING

300 g raspberry purée
50 g still mineral water
90 g light brown sugar
24 g glucose syrup
4 g pectin NH

In a saucepan, bring the raspberry purée, water, 70 g of the light brown sugar and glucose syrup to the boil. Add the remaining 20 g of sugar and pectin mixed together. Allow the pectin to dissolve while stirring for about 1 minute at a gentle simmer. Leave to cool.

FOR FINISHING

Fresh raspberries (as needed)

ASSEMBLY AND FINISHING

Place a thin layer of raspberry gel on the almond and muscovado sugar fondant biscuit discs and freeze for 2 hours. Place 10 stainless steel rings, each 7 cm in diameter and 2.5 cm high, on a baking tray lined with greaseproof paper. Place the discs of sweet shortcrust pastry in the rings. Pour the raspberry crémeux to fill half the ring. Place the frozen almond and muscovado sugar fondant biscuit discs in the centre. Cover completely with raspberry cream and smooth the surface. Freeze for 4 hours.

Melt the icing at 50°C, then use it at 37°C. Unmould the rings and glaze. Leave the glossy raspberry icing to set. On the left of the cakes, place the raspberry fomico mousse quenelles and add a fresh raspberry. Refrigerate until ready to use.

Ispahan

Creating Ispahan was a real personal challenge. For this 'Fetish' collection flavour from the maison, I had to identify all its distinctive characteristics and the result is absolutely stunning. The macarons have the crunchy, chewy texture we've come to expect, and the cream is particularly tasty, making the taste of the fruit all the more intense.

Pierre Hermé

Makes 10 individual cakes

Preparation time: 6 hours
Resting time: 13 hours
Cooking time: 15-20 minutes

FOR THE LYCHEES IN SYRUP (PREPARE THE DAY BEFORE)
150 g lychees in syrup

Drain the lychees. Cut into halves or thirds depending on the size of the fruit and leave to drain overnight in the fridge.

FOR THE PINK MACARON SHELL
250 g ground almonds
250 g icing sugar
A few drops of natural red food colouring
245 g still mineral water
14 g potato protein
250 g caster sugar

Mix the ground almonds and icing sugar in equal parts, and add the food colouring.

Mix 90 g water and 5 g potato protein, then add to the previous mixture. In a saucepan, heat the sugar and 65 g water to 118°C, checking using a thermometer or electronic probe. Mix the remaining water with the remaining potato protein. When the sugar reaches 110°C, whisk the water/potato protein mixture to thicken. Once the mixture forms soft peaks, but is not too stiff, set the food processor to speed 2, pour in the sugar syrup and blend. Leave to cool to around 35-40°C, then remove the bowl from the processor. Stir the meringue into the food colouring/water/protein mixture. Allow the mixture to deflate and transfer to a piping bag.

ASSEMBLY AND COOKING

Using a pasty bag fitted with a plain No. 11 tip, pipe 20 macarons 7 cm in diameter onto a baking tray lined with greaseproof paper. Leave the macarons to rest and form a skin at room temperature for 30-45 minutes. Bake in a fan oven at 165°C for 15-20 minutes, opening the oven door twice quickly to let the moisture escape. Leave to cool on the baking tray. Transfer to a wire rack and leave to cool completely.

FOR THE ITALIAN MERINGUE

180 g still mineral water
10 g pea protein
0.25 g xanthan gum
235 g caster sugar

Using an immersion blender, mix 105 g of the water, the pea protein and the xanthan gum together. Leave to rest for 20 minutes in the fridge before whipping the mixture at medium speed in the bowl of a food processor fitted with a whisk attachment. In a saucepan, heat the remaining water and sugar to 121°C, checking using a thermometer or electronic probe. Drizzle the sugar syrup over the water/protein/xanthan mixture. Leave to cool, blending at the same speed.

Note: once the meringue has cooled, it is best to let it run on low speed rather than letting it set, to improve the result and hold.

FOR THE ROSE PETAL CREAM

230 g Italian meringue
250 g margarine
2.7 g natural rose flavouring
A few drops of natural red food colouring

In the bowl of a food processor fitted with a whisk attachment, cream the margarine at room temperature and then fold in the Italian meringue by hand. Whisk the resulting mixture to make it light and creamy. Once the cream is smooth and homogeneous, add the natural rose flavouring and colouring and mix. Use immediately or keep refrigerated in an airtight container.

ASSEMBLY AND FINISHING
Glucose syrup (as needed)
350-400 g fresh raspberries
10 red rose petals

On a baking tray lined with greaseproof paper, place 10 pink macarons, turned upside down. Using a piping bag fitted with a plain No. 10 tip, fill them with a spiral of rose petal cream, place the raspberries in a crown following the outside diameter of the pink macaron so that they are visible. Place the drained lychees in the centre, top with more cream and place the remaining pink macarons on top. Press lightly. Set the Ispahan aside in the fridge for 1 hour. Decorate with red rose petals, a drop of glucose syrup dew made with a paper cone, and fresh raspberries. Keep in the fridge until ready to use.

FRUIT DESSERTS AND TARTS   *Fruity and sweet*

Victoria pavlova

I was inspired by a combination of coconut, pineapple and lime that I came up with at the end of the 1980s. I then gradually developed it by adding black pepper and coriander leaves. The challenge here was to get the texture of the meringue right, both in terms of the recipe development and cooking. Bringing out the full flavour of the coconut, using a non-deodorised coconut oil was a success.

Pierre Hermé

Makes 10 individual pavlovas

Preparation time: 6 hours
Resting time: 12 hours
Cooking time: 2 hours

FOR THE ALBA CREAM (PREPARE THE DAY BEFORE)
200 g soya milk
200 g non-deodorised coconut oil
2 g xanthan gum

In a saucepan, heat the soya milk to 45°C, checking using a thermometer or electronic probe. Pour the hot milk over the non-deodorised coconut oil and then add the xanthan gum. Using an immersion blender, blend to an emulsion. The mixture should be between 35-40°C. Pour into a casserole dish, cover with cling film in direct contact, leave to cool and leave to set in the fridge for around 12 hours.

FOR THE COCONUT AND LIME MERINGUE
1 g organic lime zest
6 g potato protein
0.8 g fine salt
1.2 g xanthan gum
118 g still mineral water
240 g caster sugar
34 g potato starch
Dessicated coconut (as needed)

Using a Microplane® grater, grate the lime zest. Using an immersion blender, mix the potato protein, salt, xanthan gum and water together. Pour the mixture into the bowl of a food processor fitted with a whisk attachment and whip to a soft meringue, adding the sugar gradually. Using a spatula, stir in the potato starch and lime zest mixed together. Use immediately.

Using a piping bag fitted with a No. 15 plain tip, pipe 6 cm diameter meringue balls onto a baking tray lined with greaseproof paper. Dust lightly with the dessicated coconut. Bake in a fan oven at 100°C for around 2 hours, opening the oven door twice quickly to let the moisture escape. Leave to cool. Cover with cling film and set aside at room temperature.

Note: the 2-hour baking time is a guide only and may vary depending on the oven. The meringues should be crisp.

FOR THE COCONUT PASTRY CREAM

17 g cornflour
95 g oat milk
110 g coconut purée
30 g caster sugar
2.5 g margarine

Sift the cornflour. In a saucepan, bring the oat milk and coconut purée to the boil with 10 g of sugar. Mix the cornflour and the remaining sugar. Mix this mixture in two batches to the oat milk/coconut mixture. Bring the pastry cream to the boil, whisking briskly. Remove from the heat, add the margarine, and mix. Place in a casserole dish, cover with cling film in direct contact and leave to cool. Set aside in the fridge.

FOR THE COCONUT AND LIME CREAM

125 g coconut pastry cream
Zest of ½ organic lime
250 g alba cream

Using a Microplane® grater, grate the lime zest. In the bowl of a food processor fitted with a whisk attachment, whip the alba cream. Using a whisk, smooth the pastry cream, add the lime zest and then, using a spatula, fold in the whipped alba cream. Use immediately.

Note: alba cream is a very firm cream. Be careful not to over whip it.

FOR THE EXOTIC COATING
100 g still mineral water
Zest of ¼ organic orange
Zest of ½ organic lemon
½ vanilla pod, split and scraped
80 g caster sugar
8 g pectin NH
8 g organic lemon juice
2 fresh mint leaves, coarsely chopped

Using a vegetable peeler, remove the citrus zest. In a saucepan, heat the water, zest and split vanilla pod to 45°C, checking using a thermometer or electronic probe. Add the sugar mixed with the pectin and bring to the boil for 3 minutes. Remove from the heat, add the lemon juice and fresh mint, stir and leave to infuse for 30 minutes before straining. Use immediately or leave to cool and set aside in the fridge.

FOR THE COATED PINEAPPLE
500 g ripe pineapple
5 g fresh coriander leaves, chopped
A few turns of freshly ground Sarawak black pepper
Zest of ½ organic lime
50 g exotic icing

Using a Microplane® grater, grate the lime zest. Using a chopping board and a knife, remove both ends and the skin from the pineapple before cutting the fruit into sticks, 3 cm long and 5 mm thick. Place them in a stainless steel bowl, add the remaining ingredients and the exotic coating, heated to 35°C, and mix gently. Use immediately.

FOR THE ASSEMBLY
30 fresh coriander leaves

Place the meringues, upside down, in the centre of the plates. Using a piping bag fitted with a No. 15 plain tip, pipe a ball of coconut-lime cream. Using a 6 cm diameter biscuit cutter placed on the meringue, arrange the coated pineapple sticks. Garnish with 3 fresh coriander leaves and serve immediately, as the meringue will soften very quickly.

Atlas garden baba

For the Atlas garden baba, I chose to create an alcohol-free recipe right from the start. So I needed a syrup with character. I decided to use honey from the Corsican maquis for its distinctive flavour. I've always advocated the idea of doing things differently, of learning, of opening up to other cultures and other techniques, but never to the detriment of taste. So honey makes an appearance in this baba!

Pierre Hermé

Makes 10 individual babas

Preparation time: 6 hours
Resting time: 24 hours
Cooking time: 30 minutes

FOR THE BABA DOUGH (PREPARE 2 DAYS BEFORE SOAKING)
30 g deodorised coconut oil
10 g fresh yeast
150 g still mineral water
190 g T45 flour
30 g caster sugar
2.5 g Guérande fleur de sel

Melt the deodorised coconut oil and store at 30–35°C. In the bowl of a food processor fitted with a dough hook or a flat beater attachment for small quantities, dilute the yeast in three quarters of the water, then add the flour and sugar. Mix on speed 1 until the dough is smooth, then switch to speed 2 until the dough is smooth and not sticky and add the rest of the water. Process until the dough begins to come away from the sides of the bowl and reaches a temperature of 25°C. Add the deodorised coconut oil heated to 25°C, and the fleur de sel. Process the dough on speed 2 until it comes loose and slaps against the sides of the bowl (temperature: 26°C). Using a cooking spray, grease ten 7 cm diameter savarin moulds and, using a piping bag without a tip, fill them a third of the way up. Tap the moulds well to remove as many air bubbles as possible. Leave to rise at 32°C for 45 minutes. Bake in a fan oven at 170°C for 20 minutes, turn out and return to the oven for a further 10 minutes. Leave to dry for 2 days at room temperature. Store in an airtight container.

Note: the babas need to be very dry to absorb as much syrup as possible, so that they melt in the mouth.

FOR THE HOMEMADE SEMI-CONFIT LEMONS AND ORANGES (PREPARE THE DAY BEFORE)

2 organic lemons
1 organic orange
1 kg still mineral water
500 g caster sugar

Using a serrated knife, cut off both ends of the citrus fruit and then quarter them from top to bottom. Blanch them three times; immerse them into plenty of boiling water, leave to boil for 2 minutes, then rinse in cold water. Repeat the process twice and drain. Prepare a syrup with the sugar and water and bring to the boil. Add the citrus fruit and simmer over a low heat, with a lid to preserve the softness, for around 2 hours. Remove and leave to macerate overnight in the fridge before draining with a sieve for 1 hour. Set aside separately in the fridge.

FOR THE POACHED AND BLENDED ORANGE SLICES (PREPARE THE DAY BEFORE)

500 g still mineral water
250 g caster sugar
150 g organic orange slices

Boil the water and sugar in a saucepan.

Use a knife to cut the oranges into 2 mm thick slices. Place in a casserole dish to a maximum thickness of 1.5 cm. Pour over the boiling syrup and leave to macerate for 24 hours. Drain and blend in a food processor.

FOR THE ORANGE AND LEMON COMPOTE (PREPARE THE DAY BEFORE)

30 g caster sugar
5.5 g pectin 325 NH 95
60 g organic lemon juice
3 g organic orange zest
140 g organic orange slices, poached and blended

In a mixing bowl, combine the sugar and pectin. Using a thermometer or electronic probe to check the temperature, heat the juice, zest and slices of poached and blended oranges in a saucepan to 40°C. Add the sugar/pectin mixture and bring to the boil. Pour the orange and lemon compote into a casserole dish lined with cling film, then leave to cool in the fridge for at least 12 hours. Cut into 1 cm cubes and freeze. Store in an airtight container in the freezer.

FRUIT DESSERTS AND TARTS *Fruity and sweet*

FOR THE ALBA CREAM
(PREPARE THE DAY BEFORE)
200 g soya milk
200 g deodorised coconut oil
0.4 g xanthan gum

In a saucepan, heat the soya milk to 45°C, checking using a thermometer or electronic probe. Pour the hot milk over the deodorised coconut oil and the xanthan gum. Using an immersion blender, blend to an emulsion. The mixture should be between 35-40°C. Pour into a stainless steel candissoire, cover with cling film in direct contact, leave to cool and leave to set in the fridge for around 12 hours.

FOR THE SOAKING SYRUP
(PREPARE THE DAY BEFORE)
650 g still mineral water
260 g Corsican maquis honey
10.5 g organic lemon zest
10.5 g organic orange zest
105 g organic lemon juice

Using a peeler, remove the zest from the citrus fruit and put it in the water with the honey. Bring to the boil and leave to infuse overnight in the fridge. Then add the citrus juice and strain. Use immediately at 50°C or leave to cool and set aside in the fridge.

SOAKING THE BABAS

Pour soaking syrup at 50°C into a large container and add the babas. Place a wire rack or weight to keep the babas submerged and leave overnight in the fridge. Once the babas are soaked, remove with a slotted spoon and place on a wire rack over a baking tray. Leave to drain in the fridge for 2 hours.

FOR THE ORANGE BLOSSOM
PASTRY CREAM
25 g cornflour
200 g oat milk
40 g caster sugar
Zest of ¼ organic orange
50 g margarine
2 g natural orange flower flavouring

Sift the cornflour. In a saucepan, bring the oat milk to the boil with a third of the sugar and the orange zest. Mix the cornflour and the remaining sugar. Mix this mixture with half the oat milk/sugar/orange zest mixture before adding it to the rest. Bring the pastry cream to the boil, whisking briskly. Remove from the heat, add the margarine and natural orange blossom flavouring, mix and leave to cool. Use immediately or keep refrigerated.

FOR THE ORANGE BLOSSOM CREAM
165 g orange blossom pastry cream
335 g alba cream

In the bowl of a food processor fitted with a whisk attachment, whip the alba cream. Using a whisk, smooth the orange blossom pastry cream, then using a spatula, fold in the whipped alba cream. Use immediately.

Note: alba cream is a very firm cream. Be careful not to over whip it.

FOR THE CREAMY HONEY
266 g Corsican maquis honey
110 g margarine

Whisk the margarine in the bowl of a food processor fitted with a whisk, then add the honey. Use immediately.

ASSEMBLY AND FINISHING
150 g neutral glaze
2 organic lemons

Brush the cold babas with the warm neutral glaze. Place them on plates. Garnish the base of the babas with the creamy honey, then sprinkle with the orange and lemon compote cubes. Add lemon segments. Using a piping bag fitted with an F7 chantilly tip, pipe a rosette of orange blossom cream. Garnish with 2 slices of homemade semi-confit lemon (1 cm) and 1 slice of homemade semi-confit orange (2.5 cm). Keep in the fridge until ready to use.

Fraisier cake

The fraisier has always been my favourite cake. I made this version by combining the almond paste with the leonard biscuit and alba cream.

Linda Vongdara

Serves 6-8

Preparation time: 6 hours
Resting time: 14 hours
Cooking time: 10 minutes

FOR THE VANILLA ALBA CREAM (PREPARE THE DAY BEFORE)
1 Tahiti vanilla pod
220 g soya milk
135 g deodorised coconut oil
35 g light brown sugar
10 g cornflour
100 g margarine at room temperature

Split the vanilla pod in half and scrape out the seeds. Mix with 125 g of soya milk and the deodorised coconut oil and bring to the boil. Cover and leave to infuse for 15 minutes. Remove the pod and leave the mixture to cool to 30°C. Emulsify with an immersion blender for 1-2 minutes until smooth and homogeneous, white and opaque. Place this first emulsion in the fridge to use at 7°C.

In a small saucepan, stir together the light brown sugar, cornflour and remaining soya milk. Bring to the boil to thicken, then remove from the heat and add the margarine, emulsifying the hot mixture with an immersion blender. Leave this second emulsion to cool and place in the fridge for 12 hours to set.

Make the alba cream: in the bowl of a food processor fitted with a whisk attachment, whip the first emulsion at 7°C until it forms a firm chantilly cream. Using a whisk, whip the second emulsion to soften it, then add it gradually, in three stages, to the bowl of the food processor. The cream should have a satiny texture and remain firm but supple. Pour the alba cream into a piping bag and use immediately.

FOR THE LEONARD BISCUIT WITH LEMON ZEST

95 g light brown sugar
145 g soya milk
120 g T45 fine wheat flour
30 g cornflour
60 g ground almonds
5 g lemon zest
10 g baking powder
8 g ground chia seeds
50 g deodorised coconut oil
50 g olive oil
40 g flaked almonds
80 g white chocolate

In the bowl of a food processor fitted with a flat beater attachment, blend the light brown sugar and soya milk until the sugar has completely dissolved. Add the flour, cornflour, ground almonds, lemon zest, baking powder and chia seeds all at once and mix well to obtain a smooth dough. Leave the mixture to hydrate and thicken for at least 20 minutes. Gently melt the deodorised coconut oil in a saucepan over a low heat and add the olive oil. Allow the oil mixture to come to room temperature. Preheat the fan oven to 200°C.

After resting, emulsify the dough with the oils poured gradually into the bowl of a food processor, on medium speed, until you obtain a smooth dough. Pour the dough onto a 40 x 30 cm baking tray lined with greaseproof paper and smooth the surface with an offset spatula. Cover with flaked almonds. Bake in a fan oven for 10 minutes until golden brown on the surface. When cooked, leave to cool and remove the greaseproof paper. Cut out a 16 cm diameter disc and an 12 cm diameter disc. Melt the white chocolate and butter in a bain-marie. Cover the 16 cm disc with the white chocolate to keep the flaked almonds crunchy.

FOR THE VANILLA SOAKING SYRUP

250 g still mineral water
125 g caster sugar
1 Tahiti vanilla pod
1 g agar-agar

Split the vanilla pod in half and scrape out the seeds. In a small saucepan, bring the water, vanilla, sugar and agar-agar to the boil. Use the syrup, while still warm and before it sets, to soak the 2 biscuit discs (12 and 16 cm in diameter) with a brush, soaking only the side without white chocolate for the 16 cm disc.

FOR THE STRAWBERRY CONFIT

200 g fresh strawberries
30 g caster sugar
4 g pectin NH
190 g strawberry purée
10 g lemon juice

Cut the strawberries into 1 cm cubes and set aside in the fridge. Mix the pectin with 15 g of sugar and set aside. In a small saucepan, whisk together the strawberry purée, lemon juice and remaining sugar. Bring everything to the boil. Sprinkle in the sugar and pectin mixture and stir and boil for 1 minute. Remove from the heat and add the strawberry cubes. Place the strawberry confit in a piping bag without a tip in the fridge.

ASSEMBLY AND FINISHING
150 g fresh strawberries
180 g almond paste (50% almonds)

Trim the ends of the strawberries (the part with the leaf) so that they are all the same height. Cut them in half lengthwise. Place a 16 cm diameter, 4 cm high stainless steel dessert ring on a baking tray lined with greaseproof paper; place a 4 cm high strip of plastic around the edge. Place the 16 cm diameter previously soaked biscuit disc on the bottom with the flaked almonds. Place the strawberry halves on top to cover the disc, taking care to press the cut side of the fruit lightly against the plastic strip. Fill one third high with the vanilla alba cream. Garnish with strawberry confit and top with a little alba cream. Place the second previously soaked leonard biscuit on top and cover it completely with the alba cream. Smooth the surface with a spatula and set aside in the fridge for at least 2 hours. Knead the almond paste and spread thinly between two plastic sheets, to about 2 mm thick. Peel off the sheets and lightly fold the almond paste into irregular drapes. Cut out a circle 16 cm in diameter and place the lightly folded almond paste over the surface of the fraisier. Use a blow torch to lightly brown and decorate with whole fresh strawberries. Remove the stainless steel ring and the plastic strip. Enjoy chilled.

Note: alba cream is a vegan whipped cream, the base of which is usually an emulsion made from one third deodorised coconut oil and one third soya milk, whipped into a chantilly and then finished with one third pastry cream. In this slightly richer recipe, margarine is added to help the cake hold together better.

Ispahan baba

Babas are one of my firm favourites. I was blown away by the dazzling precision and purity of their taste. As for the texture, light and moist, it's reminiscent of everything we love in a baba. The icing on the cake is the raspberry eau de vie!

Pierre Hermé

Serves 6-8

Preparation time: 6 hours
Resting time: 24 hours
Cooking time: 30 minutes

FOR THE BABA DOUGH (PREPARE 2 DAYS BEFORE SOAKING)

30 g deodorised coconut oil
10 g fresh yeast
190 g T45 flour
150 g still mineral water
30 g caster sugar
2.5 g Guérande fleur de sel

Melt the deodorised coconut oil and store at 30-35°C. In the bowl of a food processor fitted with a dough hook or a flat beater attachment for small quantities, dilute the yeast in three quarters of the water, then add the flour and sugar. Mix on speed 1 until the dough is smooth, then switch to speed 2 until the dough is smooth and not sticky. Add the rest of the water. Process until the dough begins to come away from the sides of the bowl and reaches a temperature of 25°C. Add the deodorised coconut oil heated to 25°C, and the fleur de sel. Process the dough on speed 2 until it comes loose and slaps against the sides of the bowl (temperature: 26°C). Using a cooking spray, grease an 18 cm diameter savarin mould. Using a piping bag without a tip, fill the mould a third of the way up, using your hands to shape the dough and making a hole in the centre before placing it in the mould. Tap the mould well to remove as many air bubbles as possible. Leave to rise at 32°C for around 45 minutes. Bake in a fan oven at 170°C for 20 minutes, turn out and return to the oven for a further 10 minutes. Leave to dry for 2 days at room temperature. Store in an airtight container.

Note: The baba must be very dry to absorb as much syrup as possible, so that it melts in the mouth.

FRUIT DESSERTS AND TARTS *Fruity and sweet*

FOR THE SMOOTH RASPBERRY CREAM
(PREPARE THE DAY BEFORE)

12 g cornflour
2.5 g pectin NH
330 g raspberry purée
60 g deodorised coconut oil
1.5 g liquid lecithin

Sift the cornflour with the NH pectin. In a saucepan, heat the raspberry purée to 40°C, checking using a thermometer or electronic probe. Whisk in the cornflour/pectin mixture vigorously, then bring to the boil. Pour over the deodorised coconut oil and lecithin. Using an immersion blender, blend to an emulsion. Place in a casserole dish, cover with cling film in direct contact and leave to cool. Leave to set in the fridge for around 12 hours.

FOR THE ALBA CREAM
(PREPARE THE DAY BEFORE)

200 g soya milk
200 g deodorised coconut oil
0.4 g xanthan gum

In a saucepan, heat the soya milk to 45°C, checking using a thermometer or electronic probe. Pour the hot milk over the deodorised coconut oil and the xanthan gum. Using an immersion blender, blend to an emulsion. The mixture should be between 35–40°C. Pour into a casserole dish, cover with cling film in direct contact and leave to cool. Leave to set in the fridge for around 12 hours.

FOR THE LYCHEES IN SYRUP
(PREPARE THE DAY BEFORE)

150 g lychees in syrup

Drain the lychees. Cut into halves or thirds depending on the size of the fruit and leave to drain overnight in the fridge.

FOR THE RASPBERRY AND ROSE BABA SOAKING SYRUP

600 g still mineral water
250 g caster sugar
100 g raspberry purée
60 g alcoholic rose extract
50 g raspberry eau de vie

In a saucepan bring the water, sugar and raspberry purée to the boil. Remove from the heat and add the alcoholic rose extract and raspberry eau de vie. Use immediately at 50°C or leave to cool and set aside in the fridge.

SOAKING THE BABA

Pour the soaking syrup at 50°C into a large container and soak the baba. Place a stainless steel wire rack or weight to keep the baba submerged and leave overnight in the fridge. Once the baba is soaked, remove using a slotted spoon and place it on a stainless steel wire rack over a baking tray. Leave to drain in the fridge for 2 hours.

FOR THE ROSE PASTRY CREAM
25 g cornflour
200 g oat milk
40 g caster sugar
50 g margarine
5.5 g alcoholic rose extract

Sift the cornflour. In a saucepan, bring the oat milk to the boil with a third of the sugar. Mix the cornflour and the remaining sugar. Mix with half the sweetened oat milk, whisking briskly. Remove from the heat, add the margarine and alcoholic rose extract, mix and leave to cool. Use immediately or keep refrigerated.

FOR THE ROSE CREAM
165 g rose pastry cream
335 g alba cream

In the bowl of a food processor fitted with a whisk attachment, whip the alba cream. Using a whisk, smooth the rose pastry cream, then using a spatula, fold in the whipped alba cream. Use immediately.

Note: alba cream is a very firm cream. Be careful not to over whip it.

ASSEMBLY AND FINISHING
100 g raspberry eau de vie
150 g neutral glaze
Glucose syrup (as needed)
3 red rose petals
3 fresh raspberries

Generously drizzle the raspberry eau de vie over the baba. Using a brush, coat the cold baba with the neutral glaze, warmed slightly. Transfer the baba to a plate. Place lychee pieces in the base of the baba and, using a piping bag fitted with a plain tip, pipe in the smooth raspberry cream. Using a piping bag fitted with a No. 20 Saint Honoré tip, pipe zigzags of rose pastry cream. Top with 3 fresh raspberries and 3 red rose petals and a dewdrop made with a cone filled with glucose syrup.

Ice creams and Sorbets

Frosted delights

While sorbets are easy to make, ice creams are a completely different matter. You need to recreate the smooth, creamy feel of ice cream. Contrary to what you might think, developing these ice creams took time and a great deal of experimentation, because we had to bring out the flavour of each ingredient through an unusual medium. The expression of taste and textures are modified.

I chose to work on two of our Fetish flavours: Ouréa and Miléna, to give us reference points for achieving the texture we're looking for. Making a vegan version of two existing frozen desserts is an extra feat, because we're setting ourselves the goal of doing just as well, if not better. Here again, the difficulty lies in replacing the incredible properties of eggs, milk and cream. The whole technique involves perfecting the emulsion to obtain the perfect, creamy texture that I like in ice creams, while bringing out the flavours. This involves combining sugars to control the sweetness, texture and creaminess of the ice cream. The trick is then to find the right balance between these sugars, vegetable fats — deodorised coconut oil, for example — vegan milks, thickeners and the citrus fibres that link the ingredients together. Taking a different approach to ice-cream making means constantly pushing back the boundaries of creativity.

The special feature of our ice creams is their marbling, which means that each mouthful is perceived in a different way. I use this principle for all my ice creations, layering the different flavours, measuring and weighing each layer, then mixing them with an ice-cream scoop. I kept the same approach for these vegan versions.

Here again, I'm not looking to compare, but to draw out the positive side of each creation, to discover other emotions, other sensations, with pleasure as my only guide.

Infinitely coconut ice cream

The difficulty in making ice creams is finding the right balance of ingredients and sugar, and the perfect emulsion to get the creamy texture I like. Infinitely coconut ice cream goes perfectly with chunks of fresh pineapple, which can be seasoned with lime zest and chopped coriander leaves or with caramelised pineapple.

Pierre Hermé

Makes 2 litres of ice cream

Preparation time: 2 hours
Resting time: 5 hours
Cooking time: 12-15 minutes

FOR THE INFINITELY COCONUT ICE CREAM

35 g dessicated coconut
720 g coconut milk
400 g coconut purée
4 g citrus fibre
150 g caster sugar
42 g dextrose
70 g glucose powder
50 g inverted sugar
30 g deodorised coconut oil
2 g guar gum
2 g carob bean gum

Preheat the oven to 150°C.
Spread the dessicated coconut on a baking tray lined with greaseproof paper and bake for 12-15 minutes. Remove from the oven and leave to cool completely.
In a saucepan, combine the coconut milk with the coconut purée. At 25°C, add the citrus fibre. At 30°C, add 125 g of the sugar, the dextrose, glucose powder and inverted sugar. At 40°C, add the deodorised coconut oil, previously melted at 40°C. At 45°C, add the guar gum, carob bean gum and remaining sugar. Cook the mixture at 85°C, checking using a thermometer or electronic probe, for 2 minutes. Using an immersion blender, blend the mixture. Leave to cool to 4°C, then leave to stand for at least 4 hours before churning.
Place a stainless steel tray in the freezer for 30 minutes. Using an immersion blender, blend the ice cream a second time. Churn. Once out of the ice-cream maker, pour the ice cream into the stainless steel tray, sprinkle with the toasted coconut and set aside in the freezer. Refrigerate for 30 minutes before use.

Note: be careful to add the ingredients at the correct temperatures.

Infinitely hazelnut praline ice cream

Building on our work on Ouréa and Miléna, I set myself the challenge of making our Infinitely hazelnut ice cream, a particularly creamy and fragrant creation. The flavoursome marbling is made by superimposing the ice cream, praline and hazelnut coulis.

Pierre Hermé

Makes 2 litres of ice cream

Preparation time: 6 hours
Resting time: 5 hours
Cooking time: 15 minutes

FOR THE CARAMELISED AND CRUSHED PIEDMONT HAZELNUTS
140 g unpeeled Piedmont hazelnuts
500 g caster sugar
150 g still mineral water

On a baking tray lined with greaseproof paper, spread out the hazelnuts, taking care that they don't overlap. Roast them in a fan oven at 165°C for 15 minutes. Remove the skin by passing them through a large-mesh sieve. In a saucepan, heat the water and sugar to 118°C, checking using a thermometer or electronic probe, then add the warm hazelnuts. Caramelise over a low heat. Pour the caramelised hazelnuts onto a baking tray lined with a non-stick silicone mat. Let cool and crush. Store in an airtight container.

FOR THE HOMEMADE HAZELNUT PRALINE

160 g whole hazelnuts, without skins
100 g caster sugar
30 g still mineral water
1 Madagascar vanilla pod

On a baking tray lined with greaseproof paper, spread out the hazelnuts, taking care that they don't overlap. Bake in a fan oven at 160°C for 15 minutes. Cook the sugar and water in a saucepan until a thermometer or electronic probe reads 121°C. Pour the hot syrup over the split and scraped vanilla pod and the warm roasted hazelnuts. Mix gently with a wooden spatula, then leave to caramelise over a medium heat. Transfer to a non-stick silicone mat to cool. Coarsely crush the caramelised hazelnuts and place them in the bowl of a food processor. Mix to obtain a paste that should not be too finely ground. Use immediately or keep refrigerated.

Note: caramelised hazelnuts must be crushed, ground and used as soon as they have cooled. Once they have been caramelised, they must not be stored as they can absorb moisture and this may alter the quality of the praline.

FOR THE HAZELNUT PRALINE COULIS

90 g still mineral water
65 g glucose syrup
40 g dextrose
115 g homemade hazelnut praline
115 g pure roasted hazelnut paste (100% hazelnuts)

Bring the water, glucose syrup and dextrose to the boil in a saucepan. Pour over the homemade hazelnut praline and the pure hazelnut paste, previously mixed together. Blend with an immersion blender to emulsify and set aside in the fridge.

FOR THE PRALINE ICE CREAM

700 g oat milk
30 g inulin
65 g caster sugar
35 g glucose powder
25 g inverted sugar
42 g deodorised coconut oil
1.5 g guar gum
1.5 g carob bean gum
3 g citrus fibre
130 g hazelnut praline (65% hazelnuts)

Pour the oat milk into a saucepan. At 25°C, add the inulin. At 30°C, add 50 g of the sugar, the glucose powder and the inverted sugar. At 40°C, add the deodorised coconut oil, previously melted at 40°C. At 45°C, add the guar gum, carob bean gum, citrus fibre and remaining sugar. Cook the mixture at 85°C for 2 minutes, checking using a thermometer or electronic probe, then pour over the hazelnut praline. Using an immersion blender, blend the mixture and leave to cool to 4°C. Leave to stand for at least 4 hours before churning.

Note: be careful to add the ingredients at the correct temperatures.

FOR THE INFINITELY HAZELNUT PRALINE ICE CREAM MIXTURE

175 g crushed caramelised hazelnuts
1 kg praline ice cream
260 g hazelnut praline coulis

Place a stainless steel tray containing the caramelised and crushed Piedmont hazelnuts in the freezer for 30 minutes. Using an immersion blender, blend the ice cream a second time. Churn.

Once out of the ice-cream maker, pour the ice cream into the stainless steel tray and leave in the freezer for 30 minutes, then add the hazelnut praline coulis. Mix with a spatula or spoon to marble. Put in the freezer and refrigerate 30 minutes before use.

Infinitely Madagascar vanilla ice cream

While I usually use a combination of three vanillas (Madagascar, Tahiti and Mexico) to create my vanilla flavour, for this creation I chose to use only Madagascar vanilla, the woody notes of which are enhanced by the absence of ingredients of animal origin.

Pierre Hermé

Makes 2 litres of ice cream

Preparation time: 2 hours
Resting time: 5 hours
Cooking time: 15 minutes

FOR THE INFINITELY VANILLA ICE CREAM
815 g oat milk
6 Madagascar vanilla pods
40 g inulin
150 g caster sugar
80 g inverted sugar
120 g deodorised coconut oil
3 g citrus fibre
1.5 g guar gum
1.5 g carob bean gum

Pour the oat milk into a saucepan and bring to the boil. Add the split and scraped vanilla pods and leave to infuse for 30 minutes, then strain. Pour the vanilla-infused oat milk into a saucepan and heat. At 25°C, add the inulin. At 30°C, add 125 g of the sugar and the inverted sugar. At 40°C, add the deodorised coconut oil, previously melted at 40°C. At 45°C, add the guar gum, carob bean gum, citrus fibre and remaining sugar. Cook the mixture at 85°C, checking using a thermometer or electronic probe, for 2 minutes. Using an immersion blender, blend the mixture. Leave to cool to 4°C, then leave to stand for at least 4 hours before churning.

Place a stainless steel tray in the freezer for 30 minutes. Using an immersion blender, blend the ice cream a second time. Churn. Once out of the ice-cream maker, pour the ice cream into the stainless steel tray and set aside in the freezer. Refrigerate for 30 minutes before use.

Note: be careful to add the ingredients at the correct temperatures.

Ouréa sorbet

For ice creams, the challenge is to replace the eggs, milk and cream without losing the creaminess. The acidity, fragrance and aromas must find their expression through a vegan medium. In this version, the creamy texture of hazelnut ice cream is accompanied by the lively, fragrant notes of yuzu.

Pierre Hermé

Makes 2 litres of sorbet

Preparation time: 6 hours
Resting time: 5 hours
Cooking time: 15 minutes

FOR THE CARAMELISED PIEDMONT HAZELNUTS

140 g unpeeled Piedmont hazelnuts
500 g caster sugar
150 g still mineral water

On a baking tray lined with greaseproof paper, spread out the hazelnuts, taking care that they don't overlap. Roast them in a fan oven at 165°C for 15 minutes. Remove the skin by passing them through a large-mesh sieve. In a saucepan, heat the water and sugar to 118°C, checking using a thermometer or electronic probe, then add the warm hazelnuts. Caramelise over a low heat. Pour the caramelised hazelnuts onto a baking tray lined with a non-stick silicone mat. Let cool and crush. Store in an airtight container.

FOR THE HOMEMADE HAZELNUT PRALINE

160 g whole hazelnuts, without skins
100 g caster sugar
30 g still mineral water
1 Madagascar vanilla pod

On a baking tray lined with greaseproof paper, spread out the hazelnuts, taking care that they don't overlap. Bake in a fan oven at 160 °C for 15 minutes. Cook the sugar and water in a saucepan until a thermometer or electronic probe reads 121°C. Pour the hot syrup over the split and scraped vanilla pod and the warm roasted hazelnuts. Mix gently with a wooden spatula, then leave to caramelise over a medium heat. Transfer to a non-stick silicone mat to cool. Coarsely crush the caramelised hazelnuts and place them in the bowl of a food processor. Mix to obtain a paste that should not be too finely ground. Use immediately or keep refrigerated.

(Cont.)

Note: caramelised hazelnuts must be crushed, ground and used as soon as they have cooled. Once they have been caramelised, they must not be stored as they can absorb moisture and this may alter the quality of the praline.

FOR THE HAZELNUT PRALINE COULIS

90 g still mineral water
65 g glucose syrup
40 g dextrose
115 g homemade hazelnut praline
115 g pure roasted hazelnut paste (100% hazelnuts)

Bring the water, glucose syrup and dextrose to the boil in a saucepan. Pour over the homemade hazelnut praline and the pure hazelnut paste, previously mixed together. Blend with an immersion blender to emulsify and set aside in the fridge.

FOR THE OURÉA SORBET

10 g organic lemon zest
420 g caster sugar
805 g still mineral water
5 g dried yuzu powder
35 g inulin
140 g atomised glucose
3 g guar gum
3 g carob bean gum
565 g Kôchi yuzu juice
240 g crushed caramelised hazelnuts
330 g hazelnut praline coulis

Using a Microplane® grater, remove the lemon zest and mix with half of the sugar. Heat the water and sugar mixed with the zest, yuzu powder, atomised glucose and inulin to 45°C in a saucepan, checking using a thermometer or electronic probe. Then add the guar gum and carob bean gum mixed with the remaining sugar. Cook the mixture at 85°C, checking using a thermometer or electronic probe, for 2 minutes. Using an immersion blender, blend the mixture and leave to cool to 4°C. Leave to stand for at least 4 hours in the fridge before churning. Add the yuzu juice and blend again. Place a stainless steel tray with the caramelised and crushed hazelnuts in the freezer for 30 minutes. Then churn the yuzu sorbet, pour it into the stainless steel tray and mix lightly. Put the tray back in the freezer for 30 minutes, then spread the hazelnut praline coulis over it. Put the tray back in the freezer for 30 minutes and mix with a spatula or spoon to marble. Store in the freezer and refrigerate 30 minutes before use.

Miléna ice cream

For this interpretation of Miléna, the sorbet was easy. The mint ice cream, on the other hand, is a more difficult exercise in style, in which the unique flavour of fresh mint is sought without the support of animal fats. The marbling of the sorbet and ice cream then gives it all its uniqueness.

Pierre Hermé

Makes 2 litres of ice cream

Preparation time: 4 hours
Resting time: 5 hours
Cooking time: 15 minutes

FOR THE RED BERRY SORBET
115 g still mineral water
225 g caster sugar
50 g atomised glucose
3 g guar gum
3 g carob bean gum
540 g strawberry purée
180 g raspberry purée
90 g blackcurrant purée
90 g redcurrant purée

Pour the water and 175 g of sugar mixed with the atomised glucose into a saucepan and heat to 45°C, checking using a thermometer or electronic probe. At 45°C, add the guar gum and carob bean gum mixed with the remaining sugar. Cook the mixture at 85°C, checking using a thermometer or electronic probe, for 2 minutes. Using an immersion blender, blend the mixture and leave to cool to 4°C. Leave to stand for at least 4 hours in the fridge before churning. Add the fruit purées and blend again.

FOR THE FRESH MINT ICE CREAM

815 g oat milk
45 g fresh mint leaves, chopped
40 g inulin
150 g caster sugar
80 g inverted sugar
120 g deodorised coconut oil
1.5 g guar gum
1.5 g carob bean gum
3 g citrus fibre

Bring 400 g of oat milk to the boil in a saucepan, then infuse with the chopped fresh mint leaves for 10 minutes. Strain and top up if necessary with oat milk to reach the initial weight (400 g). Pour 415 g of cold oat milk and the infused milk into a saucepan. At 25°C, add the inulin. Warm slightly, then at 30°C, add 120 g of sugar and the inverted sugar. At 40°C, add the deodorised coconut oil, previously melted at 40°C. At 45°C, add the guar gum, carob bean gum and citrus fibre plus 30 g sugar. Cook the mixture at 85°C, checking using a thermometer or electronic probe, for 2 minutes. Using an immersion blender, blend the mixture and leave to cool to 4°C. Leave to stand for at least 4 hours before churning.

Note: be careful to add the ingredients at the correct temperatures.

FOR THE MILÉNA ICE CREAM

15 g fresh mint leaves

Place a stainless steel tray in the freezer for 30 minutes. Blanch the fresh mint leaves by immersing them in simmering water, then removing them and immersing them into iced water. Blend them in a food processor, add them to the fresh mint ice cream above and, using an immersion blender, blend a second time.

Churn the fresh mint ice cream. Once out of the ice-cream maker, pour the ice cream into the stainless steel tray and set aside in the freezer. Churn the red berry sorbet and spread over the fresh mint ice cream. Mix with a spatula or spoon to marble.

Put in the freezer and refrigerate 30 minutes before use.

Macarons

A couple of grams of happiness

How could I not dedicate a chapter to the macaron, these couple of grams of happiness, this common thread running through my creations, which I couldn't do without?

The vegan approach offered me a new playground and a new interpretation of this bite-size delight that lends itself to limitless creativity. Imagining the perfect macaron takes on its full meaning here. As well as the unique flavours and combinations that can be created, our major challenge was to make the macaron shells without egg white. We had to reproduce the crunchy, soft texture of the shell. After many attempts, we decided to use potato protein, which gives more convincing results, is easier to reproduce in terms of texture than chickpea water and is more practical for producing large quantities. To achieve the right consistency, cooking is then essential.

The garnishes, on the other hand, are easier to interpret in the vegan macarons. Margarine, vegan milks and oils combined with quality ingredients chosen for their taste make it possible to create all sorts of infinitely tasty preparations.

Plants have become a source of inspiration, allowing these new macarons to become part of the Pierre Hermé Paris collections. I invite all fans to share the emotions these unique creations inspire.

Infinitely chocolate macaron

I couldn't imagine these couple of grams of happiness without finding the texture of the biscuit and the crunch of the crust coupled with an excellent filling. For the chocolate cream, the oat milk and chocolate fats were enough to magnify the intensity and purity of the chocolate flavour.

Pierre Hermé

Makes approximately 72 macarons
(144 shells)

Preparation time: 3 hours
Resting time: 24 hours
Cooking time: 16 minutes

FOR THE CHOCOLATE MACARON SHELL
285 g ground almonds
285 g icing sugar
325 g still mineral water
19 g potato protein
65 g sifted cocoa powder
335 g caster sugar

Mix the ground almonds and icing sugar in equal parts.

Mix 120 g of water and 7 g of potato protein, then add this mixture to the previous mixture. Add the cocoa powder.

In a saucepan, heat the sugar and 85 g water to 118°C, checking using a thermometer or electronic probe. Mix 120 g water and 12 g potato protein. When the sugar syrup reaches 110°C, whisk the water/protein mixture in the bowl of a food processor fitted with a whisk. Once the mixture forms soft peaks, but is not too stiff, turn the mixer to speed 2 and pour in the sugar syrup. Leave to cool to around 35-40°C, then remove the bowl from the processor. Stir the meringue into the cocoa powder/water/protein mixture. Allow the mixture to deflate and transfer to a piping bag.

ASSEMBLY AND COOKING

Using a piping bag fitted with a No. 11 plain tip, pipe around 150 macaron shells, 3.5-4 cm in diameter, onto baking trays lined with greaseproof paper. Leave the macarons to rest and form a skin at room temperature for 30 minutes. Bake in a fan oven at 150°C for around 16 minutes opening the oven door twice quickly to let the moisture escape. Leave to cool on the baking tray. Transfer to a wire rack and leave to cool.

FOR THE CHOCOLATE CREAM

300 g oat or soya milk
15 g glucose syrup
375 g dark chocolate (Manjari 64% Valrhona® cocoa)
60 g peanut/rapeseed/grapeseed oil (as preferred)

Chop the dark chocolate. Bring a mixture of the oat milk/glucose syrup to the boil, then pour over the chocolate. Stir starting from the centre and working outwards. Add the oil, then using an immersion blender, blend the ganache. Transfer to a stainless steel candissoire and cover with cling film in direct contact. Leave to cool. Then leave to set in the fridge for 30 minutes before piping onto the macaron shells.

FOR THE CHOCOLATE SHARDS WITH FLEUR DE SEL

200 g dark chocolate (Manjari 64% Valrhona® cocoa)
3.6 g Guérande fleur de sel

Crush the fleur de sel with a rolling pin and sieve it through a medium/fine sieve. Use only the finest crystals from the sieve. Temper the dark chocolate to keep it shiny, smooth and stable. Chop the chocolate with a serrated knife and place in an earthenware bowl, then melt it in a bain-marie. Stir gently with a wooden spoon until it reaches 50-55°C. Remove the chocolate from the bain-marie. Place the bowl in a second bowl filled with water and 4-5 ice cubes. Stir the melted chocolate from time to time as it will start to set on the sides of the bowl. As soon as it reaches 27-28°C, return the bowl to the bain-marie, keeping a close eye on the temperature. When it reaches 31-32°C, the chocolate is tempered. Add the fleur de sel. Spread the tempered chocolate with fleur de sel over a sheet of greaseproof paper. Place a second sheet of greaseproof paper and a weight on top to prevent the chocolate from warping as it sets. Refrigerate for a few hours. Coarsely crush the fleur de sel chocolate slabs and use immediately or keep in an airtight container in the fridge.

ASSEMBLING THE MACARONS

Turn the macaron shells onto stainless steel wire racks. Using a piping bag fitted with a plain No. 11 tip, generously fill half the macaron biscuit shells with chocolate cream. Sprinkle with the fleur de sel chocolate shards in the centre. Cover with the remaining macaron shells, taking care to match the sizes of the shells. Refrigerate uncovered for at least 24 hours, but preferably 36 hours. Place the macarons in airtight containers and keep in the fridge. Remove the macarons from the fridge 2 hours before eating.

Infinitely yuzu macaron

For the yuzu macaron, making the cream was a little more complicated because, unlike chocolate, fruit juices contain no fat. So we had to develop a recipe combining vegan milks and vegetable oils, rice cream and agar-agar to tame the yuzu juice into an intensely flavoured cream.

Pierre Hermé

Makes approximately 72 macarons (144 shells)

Preparation time: 3 hours
Resting time: 36 hours
Cooking time: 16 minutes

FOR THE YUZU CREAM (PREPARE THE DAY BEFORE)
240 g caster sugar
4 g organic lemon zest
3 g agar-agar powder
50 g rice cream
180 g soya milk
300 g Kôchi yuzu juice
90 g olive oil
90 g deodorised coconut oil

Mix together the sugar, zest, agar-agar and rice cream. Pour the soya milk and yuzu juice into a saucepan, heat, and when the mixture reaches 40°C, pour in the previous mixture. Bring to the boil and pour over the olive oil and deodorised coconut oil. Using an immersion blender, blend for several minutes to emulsify. Place in a casserole dish, cover with cling film in direct contact and leave to cool and set in the fridge for around 12 hours.

Note: the yuzu juice curdles the soya milk but this doesn't affect the final cream.

FOR THE YELLOW MACARON SHELL

300 g ground almonds
300 g icing sugar
A few drops of natural yellow food colouring
295 g still mineral water
17 g potato protein
300 g caster sugar

Mix the ground almonds and icing sugar in equal parts, and add the food colouring.

Mix 110 g water and 6 g potato protein, then add to the previous mixture.

In a saucepan, heat the sugar and 75 g water to 118°C, checking using a thermometer or electronic probe. Mix 110 g water and 11 g potato protein. When the sugar syrup reaches 110°C, whisk the water/protein mixture in the bowl of a food processor fitted with a whisk. Once the mixture forms soft peaks, but is not too stiff, set the food processor to speed 2, pour in the sugar syrup and blend. Leave to cool to around 35-40°C, then remove the bowl from the processor. Stir the meringue into the food colouring/water/protein mixture. Allow the mixture to deflate and transfer to a piping bag.

ASSEMBLY AND COOKING

Using a piping bag fitted with a No. 11 plain tip, pipe around 150 macaron shells, 3.5-4 cm in diameter, onto baking trays lined with greaseproof paper. Leave the macarons to rest and form a skin at room temperature for 30 minutes. Bake in a fan oven at 150°C for around 16 minutes opening the oven door twice quickly to let the moisture escape. Leave to cool on the baking tray. Transfer to a wire rack and leave to cool.

ASSEMBLING THE MACARONS

Turn the macaron shells onto stainless steel wire racks. Using a piping bag fitted with a plain No. 11 tip, generously fill half the macaron biscuit shells with chocolate cream. Cover with the remaining macaron shells, taking care to match the sizes of the shells. Refrigerate uncovered for at least 24 hours, but preferably 36 hours. Place the macarons in airtight containers and keep in the fridge. Remove the macarons from the fridge 2 hours before eating.

Infinitely rose macaron

When it comes to vegan pâtisserie, recipes come one after the other, but they're never the same. To create the rose filling, we used margarine and Italian meringue. The secret of the cream's evanescent texture: the whisking!

Pierre Hermé

Makes approximately 72 macarons (144 shells)

Preparation time: 3 hours
Resting time: 24 hours
Cooking time: 16 minutes

FOR THE PINK MACARON SHELL
300 g ground almonds
300 g icing sugar
A few drops of natural red food colouring
295 g still mineral water
17 g potato protein
300 g caster sugar

Mix the ground almonds and icing sugar in equal parts, and add the food colouring. Mix 110 g water and 6 g potato protein, then add to the previous mixture.

In a saucepan, heat the sugar and 75 g water to 118°C, checking using a thermometer or electronic probe. Mix 110 g water and 11 g potato protein. When the sugar syrup reaches 110°C, whisk the water/protein mixture in the bowl of a food processor fitted with a whisk. Once the mixture forms soft peaks, but is not too stiff, set the food processor to speed 2, pour in the sugar syrup and blend. Leave to cool to around 35-40°C, then remove the bowl from the processor. Stir the meringue into the food colouring/water/protein mixture. Allow the mixture to deflate and transfer to a piping bag.

ASSEMBLY AND COOKING

Using a piping bag fitted with a No. 11 plain tip, pipe around 150 macaron shells, 3.5-4 cm in diameter, onto baking trays lined with greaseproof paper. Leave the macarons to rest and form a skin at room temperature for 30 minutes. Bake in a fan oven at 150°C for around 16 minutes opening the oven door twice quickly to let the moisture escape. Leave to cool on the baking tray. Transfer to a wire rack and leave to cool.

FOR THE ITALIAN MERINGUE

235 g still mineral water
13 g pea protein
0.3 g xanthan gum
315 g caster sugar

Using an immersion blender, mix 140 g of the water, the pea protein and the xanthan gum together. Leave to rest for 20 minutes in the fridge before whipping the mixture at medium speed in the bowl of a food processor fitted with a whisk attachment. In a saucepan, heat the remaining 95 g water and sugar to 121°C, checking using a thermometer or electronic probe. Drizzle the sugar syrup over the water/protein/xanthan mixture. Leave to cool, blending at the same speed.

Note: once the meringue has cooled, it is best to let it run on low speed rather than letting it set, to improve the result and hold.

FOR THE ROSE PETAL CREAM

385 g Italian meringue
415 g margarine
4.5 g alcoholic rose flavouring
A few drops of natural red food colouring

In the bowl of a food processor fitted with a whisk attachment, cream the margarine at room temperature then fold in the Italian meringue by hand. Whisk the mixture to make it light and creamy. Once the cream is smooth and homogeneous, add the alcoholic rose flavouring and colouring and mix. Use immediately or keep refrigerated in an airtight container.

ASSEMBLING THE MACARONS

Turn the macaron shells onto stainless steel wire racks. Using a piping bag fitted with a plain No. 11 tip, generously fill half the macaron biscuit shells with chocolate cream. Cover with the remaining macaron shells, taking care to match the sizes of the shells. Refrigerate uncovered for at least 24 hours, but preferably 36 hours. Place the macarons in airtight containers and keep in the fridge. Remove the macarons from the fridge 2 hours before eating.

Infinitely hazelnut praline macaron

Hazelnuts are a gourmet delight. To identify the clear taste of the nut, it is essential to blend the cream with the margarine. To heighten the flavours and create a surprise, I added a crunchy hazelnut praline to the centre of the macaron.

Pierre Hermé

Makes approximately 72 macarons (144 shells)

Preparation time: 3 hours
Resting time: 24 hours
Cooking time: 16 minutes

FOR THE HAZELNUT MACARON SHELL
300 g ground almonds
300 g icing sugar
A few drops of natural brown food colouring
295 g still mineral water
17 g potato protein
300 g caster sugar

Mix the ground almonds and icing sugar in equal parts, and add the food colouring. Mix 110 g water and 6 g potato protein, then add to the previous mixture.

In a saucepan, heat the sugar and 75 g water to 118°C, checking using a thermometer or electronic probe. Mix 110 g water and 11 g potato protein. When the sugar syrup reaches 110°C, whisk in the water/protein mixture. Once the mixture forms soft peaks, but is not too stiff, set the food processor to speed 2, pour in the sugar syrup and blend. Leave to cool to around 35-40°C, then remove the bowl from the processor. Stir the meringue into the food colouring/water/protein mixture. Allow the mixture to deflate and transfer to a piping bag.

FOR THE ASSEMBLY
Sliced unpeeled hazelnuts (as needed)

ASSEMBLY AND COOKING
Using a piping bag fitted with a No. 11 plain tip, pipe around 150 macaron shells, 3.5-4 cm in diameter, onto baking trays lined with greaseproof paper. Sprinkle the shells with sliced unpeeled hazelnuts. Leave the macarons to rest and form a skin at room temperature for 30 minutes. Bake in a fan oven at 150°C for around 16 minutes opening the oven door twice quickly to let the moisture escape. Leave to cool on the baking tray. Transfer to a wire rack and leave to cool.

FOR THE ITALIAN MERINGUE
235 g still mineral water
13 g pea protein
0.3 g xanthan gum
315 g caster sugar

Using an immersion blender, mix 140 g of the water, the pea protein and the xanthan gum together. Leave to rest for 20 minutes in the fridge before whipping the mixture at medium speed in the bowl of a food processor fitted with a whisk attachment. In a saucepan, heat the remaining 95 g water and sugar to 121°C, checking using a thermometer or electronic probe. Drizzle the sugar syrup over the water/protein/xanthan mixture. Leave to cool, blending at the same speed.

Note: once the meringue has cooled, it is best to let it run on low speed rather than letting it set, to improve the result and hold.

FOR THE HAZELNUT PRALINE CREAM
275 g Italian meringue
300 g margarine
80 g hazelnut praline (65% hazelnuts)
65 g pure roasted hazelnut paste (100% hazelnuts)

In the bowl of a food processor fitted with a whisk attachment, cream the margarine at room temperature then fold in the Italian meringue by hand. Whisk the mixture to make it light and creamy. Once the cream is homogeneous and smooth, add the praline and pure hazelnut paste, mix and use immediately or keep in an airtight container in the fridge at 4°C.

FOR THE HOMEMADE HAZELNUT PRALINE
160 g whole hazelnuts, without skins
100 g caster sugar
30 g still mineral water
1 Madagascar vanilla pod

On a baking tray lined with greaseproof paper, spread out the hazelnuts, taking care that they don't overlap. Bake in a fan oven at 160 °C for 15 minutes. Cook the sugar and water in a saucepan until a thermometer or electronic probe reads 121°C. Pour the hot syrup over the split and scraped vanilla pod and the warm roasted hazelnuts. Mix gently and leave to caramelise over a medium heat. Transfer to a non-stick silicone mat to cool. Coarsely crush the caramelised hazelnuts and place them in the bowl of a food processor. Mix to obtain a paste that should not be too finely ground. Set aside in the fridge.

Note: caramelised hazelnuts must be crushed, ground and used as soon as they have cooled. Once they have been caramelised, they must not be stored as they can absorb moisture and this may alter the quality of the praline.

FOR THE CRUNCHY, MELT-IN-THE-MOUTH PRALINE

35 g dark chocolate (Araguani 72% Valrhona® cocoa)
100 g hazelnut praline (65% hazelnuts)
100 g homemade hazelnut praline

First, temper the chocolate to keep it shiny, smooth and stable. Chop the chocolate with a serrated knife and place in an earthenware bowl, then melt it in a bain-marie. Stir gently with a wooden spoon until it reaches 50-55°C. Remove the chocolate from the bain-marie. Place the bowl in a second bowl filled with water and 4-5 ice cubes. Stir the melted chocolate from time to time as it will start to set on the sides of the bowl. As soon as it reaches 27-28°C, return the bowl to the bain-marie, keeping a close eye on the temperature. When it reaches 31-32°C, the chocolate is tempered. Add the other ingredients.

Mix and transfer to a piping bag without a tip. Use immediately.

ASSEMBLING THE MACARONS

Turn the macaron shells onto stainless steel wire racks. Using a piping bag fitted with a plain No. 11 tip, generously fill half the macaron biscuit shells with chocolate cream. Using a piping bag without a tip, pipe a little crunchy, melt-in-the-mouth praline in the centre. Cover with the remaining macaron shells, taking care to match the sizes of the shells. Refrigerate uncovered for at least 24 hours, but preferably 36 hours. Place the macarons in airtight containers and keep in the fridge. Remove the macarons from the fridge 2 hours before eating.

Rose des sables macaron

I was inspired by the flavours of the Rose des sables cake to make this macaron, a subtle combination of roasted almonds and rose-flavoured almond milk chocolate.

Pierre Hermé

Makes approximately 144 macarons (288 shells)

Preparation time: 3 hours
Resting time: 24 hours
Cooking time: 16 minutes

FOR THE PINK MACARON SHELL
300 g ground almonds
300 g icing sugar
A few drops of natural red food colouring
295 g still mineral water
17 g potato protein
300 g caster sugar

Mix the ground almonds and icing sugar in equal parts, and add the food colouring. Mix 110 g of water and 6 g of potato protein then add this mixture to the previous mixture.

In a saucepan, heat the sugar and 75 g water to 118°C, checking using a thermometer or electronic probe. Mix 110 g water and 11 g potato protein. When the sugar syrup reaches 110°C, whisk the water/protein mixture in the bowl of a food processor fitted with a whisk. Once the mixture forms soft peaks, but is not too stiff, set the food processor to speed 2, pour in the sugar syrup and blend. Leave to cool to around 35-40°C, then remove the bowl from the processor. Stir the meringue into the food colouring/water/protein mixture. Allow the mixture to deflate and transfer to a piping bag.

FOR THE MACARON SHELL

300 g ground almonds
300 g icing sugar
295 g still mineral water
17 g potato protein
300 g caster sugar

Mix the ground almonds and icing sugar in equal parts.

Mix 110 g water and 6 g potato protein, then add to the previous mixture.

In a saucepan, heat the sugar and 75 g water to 118°C, checking using a thermometer or electronic probe. Mix 110 g water and 11 g potato protein. When the sugar syrup reaches 110°C, whisk the water/protein mixture in the bowl of a food processor fitted with a whisk. Once the mixture forms soft peaks, but is not too stiff, set the food processor to speed 2, pour in the sugar syrup and blend. Leave to cool to around 35-40°C, then remove the bowl from the processor. Stir the meringue into the ground almonds/icing sugar/water/protein mixture. Allow the mixture to deflate and transfer to a piping bag.

ASSEMBLY AND COOKING

Using two piping bags fitted with No. 11 plain tips, pipe around 150 macaron shells of each colour, 3.5-4 cm in diameter, onto baking sheets lined with greaseproof paper. Leave the macarons to rest and form a skin at room temperature for 30 minutes. Bake in a fan oven at 150°C for 16 minutes opening the oven door twice quickly to let the moisture escape. Leave to cool on the baking tray. Transfer to a wire rack and leave to cool.

FOR THE ALMOND MILK CHOCOLATE AND ROSE GANACHE

390 g almond milk chocolate (Amatika 46% Valrhona® cocoa)
11.5 g pectin X58
325 g oat milk
8 g natural rose flavouring
90 g deodorised coconut oil

Chop the chocolate. Mix the pectin X58 into the oat milk using an immersion blender. Bring the oat milk/pectin mixture to the boil in a saucepan, then pour over the chocolate. Stir starting from the centre and working outwards. Add the natural rose flavouring and deodorised coconut oil, then using an immersion blender, blend the ganache. Transfer to a casserole dish and cover with cling film in direct contact. Leave to cool and set in the fridge for 20 minutes before piping the ganache directly onto the macaron shells.

(Cont.)

FOR THE HOMEMADE ALMOND PRALINE

160 g blanched white almonds
100 g caster sugar
30 g still mineral water
1 Madagascar vanilla pod

On a baking tray lined with greaseproof paper, spread out the almonds, taking care that they don't overlap. Bake in a fan oven at 160 °C for 15 minutes. Cook the sugar and water in a saucepan until a thermometer or electronic probe reads 121°C. Pour the sugar syrup over the split and scraped vanilla pod and the warm blanched and roasted almonds. Mix gently and leave to caramelise over a medium heat. Remove to a non-stick baking tray to cool. Then crush coarsely and grind in a blender to obtain a paste that should not be too finely ground. Set aside in the fridge.

Note: caramelised almonds must be crushed, ground and used as soon as they have cooled. Once they have been caramelised, they must not be stored as they can absorb moisture and this may alter the quality of the praline.

FOR THE ALMOND FONDANT PRALINE

50 g almond milk chocolate (Amatika 46% Valrhona® cocoa)
160 g homemade almond praline
80 g pure roasted almond paste (100% almonds)

Melt the almond milk chocolate, then mix with the homemade almond praline and pure almond paste. Place in a piping bag without a tip and use immediately.

ASSEMBLING THE MACARONS

Turn the macaron shells onto stainless steel wire racks. Using a piping bag fitted with a plain No. 11 tip, generously fill the pink macaron shells with almond milk chocolate and rose ganache. Using a piping bag without a tip, pipe a little almond fondant praline and a little ganache in the centre. Cover with the remaining macaron shells, taking care to match the sizes of the shells. Refrigerate uncovered for at least 24 hours, but preferably 36 hours to allow the flavours to develop. Place the macarons in airtight containers and keep in the fridge. Remove the macarons from the fridge 2 hours before eating.

Infinitely pecan macaron

The advantage of nuts is that they add flavour and fat. The challenge, however, is to bind them into a smooth cream. Citrus fibre is the solution: being neutral in flavour, it leaves plenty of room for the aromatic range of pecans and provides a texture that's easy to pipe!

Pierre Hermé

Makes approximately 72 macarons
(144 shells)

Preparation time: 3 hours
Resting time: 24 hours
Cooking time: 1 hour

FOR THE PECAN MACARON SHELLS
275 g ground almonds
275 g icing sugar
60 g ground pecan nuts
295 g still mineral water
17 g potato protein
300 g caster sugar

Mix the ground almonds, icing sugar and ground pecan nuts.

Mix 110 g water and 6 g potato protein, then add to the previous mixture.

In a saucepan, heat the sugar and 75 g water to 118°C, checking using a thermometer or electronic probe. Mix 110 g water and 11 g potato protein. When the sugar syrup reaches 110°C, whisk the water/protein mixture in the bowl of a food processor fitted with a whisk. Once the mixture forms soft peaks, but is not too stiff, set the food processor to speed 2, pour in the sugar syrup and blend. Leave to cool to around 35–40°C, then remove the bowl from the processor. Stir the meringue into the pecan nut/water/protein mixture. Allow the mixture to deflate and transfer to a piping bag.

ASSEMBLY AND COOKING

Using a piping bag fitted with a No. 11 plain tip, pipe around 150 macaron shells, 3.5–4 cm in diameter, onto baking trays lined with greaseproof paper. Leave the macarons to rest and form a skin at room temperature for 30 minutes. Bake in a fan oven at 150°C for around 16 minutes opening the oven door twice quickly to let the moisture escape. Leave to cool on the baking tray. Transfer to a wire rack and leave to cool.

FOR THE ROASTED PECAN NUTS
300 g pecan nuts

On a baking tray lined with greaseproof paper, spread out the pecan nuts, taking care that they don't overlap. Bake in a fan oven at 140 °C for 25 minutes.

FOR THE PECAN NUT CREAM
105 g ground almonds
450 g roasted pecan nuts
150 g icing sugar
3 g Guérande fleur de sel
180 g still mineral water
4.5 g citrus fibre

On a baking tray lined with greaseproof paper, sprinkle the ground almonds in a thin, even layer. Bake in a fan oven at 170 °C for 10 minutes. After removing from the oven, let cool. Using a food processor, grind the roasted pecan nuts with the icing sugar and fleur de sel to a smooth paste. Then stir in the water and citrus fibre and finish with the roasted ground almonds. Use immediately.

FOR THE HOMEMADE ALMOND PRALINE
160 g blanched white almonds
100 g caster sugar
30 g still mineral water
1 Madagascar vanilla pod

On a baking tray lined with greaseproof paper, spread out the almonds, taking care that they don't overlap. Bake in a fan oven at 160 °C for 15 minutes. Cook the sugar and water in a saucepan until a thermometer or electronic probe reads 121°C. Pour the sugar syrup over the split and scraped vanilla pod and the warm blanched and roasted almonds. Mix by stirring regularly and leave to caramelise over a medium heat. Transfer to a non-stick silicone mat to cool. Then crush coarsely and grind in a blender to obtain a paste that should not be too finely ground. Set aside in the fridge.

Note: caramelised almonds must be crushed, ground and used as soon as they have cooled. Once they have been caramelised, they must not be stored as they can absorb moisture and this may alter the quality of the praline.

FOR THE ALMOND FONDANT PRALINE
50 g almond milk chocolate (Amatika 46% Valrhona® cocoa)
160 g homemade almond praline
80 g pure almond paste (100% almonds)

Melt the almond milk chocolate in a bain-marie, then mix with the homemade almond praline and pure almond paste. Place in a piping bag without a tip and use immediately.

ASSEMBLING THE MACARONS

Turn the macaron shells onto stainless steel wire racks. Using a piping bag fitted with a No. 11 plain tip, generously fill half the macaron shells with pecan nut cream. Using a piping bag without a tip, pipe a little almond fondant praline in the centre. Cover with the remaining macaron shells, taking care to match the sizes of the shells. Refrigerate uncovered for at least 24 hours, but preferably 36 hours. Place the macarons in airtight containers and keep in the fridge. Remove the macarons from the fridge 2 hours before eating.

Plated desserts

Desserts to share... or not

In this chapter, the taste of traditional desserts is used as a guide, as a common thread that constantly reminds us that a dessert must above all inspire emotions in those tasting it. Through these creations, I've continued my work to get to grips with the world of veganism and to push gourmet pleasures ever further. On several occasions, I was struck by the finesse and lightness of the textures. The absence of butter and eggs means that the flavours are clearer, more pronounced, closer to the raw ingredient and more precise. The textures are equally varied: crispy, flaky, crumbly or melting, and they play a fundamental role in the pleasure of tasting them.

This wealth of experience has enabled us to create some classic plated desserts, such as floating islands and brioche French toast. It has also allowed me to recreate some of my own creations, such as the 2000 feuilles and the Entre dessert to share, in a new interpretation. I created the Entre collection in 2007 with the aim of moving away from the usual sharing cakes format and getting closer to restaurant desserts in a new, creative version with some very offbeat and iconoclastic flavour combinations for the time. For this vegan interpretation, I chose to use one of my Fetish flavour combinations, Félicia (hazelnut and lemon). If I had succeeded in this challenge with daring pairings, why not try it with a classic pairing using vegan ingredients? That's how I came up with the recipe for Entre Félicia, an original creation, which is minimalist in its presentation but incredibly well considered in terms of taste and texture. As for the Infinitely almond panna cotta, for me it remains the most memorable dessert in this series. Incredibly simple and easy to understand, combining almond milk, amlou and caramelised almonds on a crunchy filo pastry base, it was a revelation. Each ingredient blends in perfectly, both in terms of taste and texture. In fact, this dessert features on the menu of one of the restaurants at the La Mamounia hotel in Marrakesh.

Entre Félicia

I've always tried to move away from decoration and focus on taste and pleasure. Entre Félicia, created for this book, is a balance between my desire for gourmet sensations and sharing. Here I've tried to bring the best out of hazelnuts and lemon. It's not a dessert but an experience to be had, emotions to be shared.

Pierre Hermé

Serves 8-10

Preparation time: 6 hours
Resting time: 15 hours
Cooking time: 2 hours 40 minutes

FOR THE HOMEMADE SEMI-CONFIT LEMON (PREPARE THE DAY BEFORE)

1 organic lemon
500 g still mineral water
250 g caster sugar

Trim both ends of the lemon. Using a serrated knife, quarter from top to bottom. Blanch it three times; immerse in plenty of boiling water, leave to boil for 2 minutes, then rinse in cold water. Repeat the process twice and drain. Prepare a syrup with the sugar and water and bring to the boil. Add the lemon and simmer over a low heat, with a lid to preserve the softness, for around 2 hours. Remove and leave to macerate overnight before draining in a sieve for 1 hour. Cut into strips and set aside in the fridge.

FOR THE LEMON CREAM (PREPARE THE DAY BEFORE)

120 g caster sugar
2 g organic lemon zest
1.5 g agar-agar powder
25 g rice cream
90 g soya milk
150 g organic lemon juice
45 g olive oil
45 g deodorised coconut oil

Mix together the sugar, zest, agar-agar and rice cream. Heat the soya milk and lemon juice in a saucepan. When the mixture reaches 40°C, pour in the previous mixture. Bring to the boil and pour over the olive oil and deodorised coconut oil. Using an immersion blender, blend for several minutes to emulsify. Place in a casserole dish, cover with cling film in direct contact and leave to cool. Leave to set in the fridge for around 12 hours.

Note: the lemon juice curdles the soya milk but this doesn't affect the final cream.

FOR THE CRUSHED ROASTED PIEDMONT HAZELNUTS

200 g unpeeled Piedmont hazelnuts

On a baking tray lined with greaseproof paper, spread out the hazelnuts, taking care that they don't overlap. Roast them in a fan oven at 165°C for 15 minutes. Remove the skin by passing them through a large-mesh sieve. Using a chopping board, crush them coarsely and use immediately, or store in an airtight container at room temperature.

FOR THE HAZELNUT LEONARD BISCUIT

30 g deodorised coconut oil
70 g plain flour
5 g baking powder
17 g potato starch
90 g soya milk
45 g brown sugar
1 g Guérande fleur de sel
30 g ground hazelnuts
4 g cider vinegar
30 g peanut oil

Melt the deodorised coconut oil at 30-35°C. Sift together the flour, baking powder and potato starch. In the bowl of a food processor fitted with a flat beater attachment, combine the soya milk, brown sugar, fleur de sel, ground hazelnut and cider vinegar, then add the previous sifted mixture. Drizzle in the oils and blend until smooth. On a baking tray lined with greaseproof paper, place a 17 cm diameter ring and pour 215 g of biscuit into it and 20 g of crushed roasted hazelnuts. Bake in a fan oven at 180°C for 10-12 minutes, opening the oven door for a few seconds every 5 minutes to let the moisture escape. After removing from the oven, let cool.

FOR THE SMOOTH HAZELNUT CREAM

665 g still mineral water
6 g inverted sugar
15 g glucose syrup
15 g cocoa butter (Valrhona®)
80 g pure roasted hazelnut paste (100% hazelnuts)
45 g hazelnut praline (60-65% hazelnuts)

Heat the water to 45°C, add the inverted sugar and glucose syrup and bring to the boil. Immediately pour over a mixture of the cocoa butter, hazelnut paste and hazelnut praline in three batches, mixing after each addition. Mix until smooth. Place in a casserole dish, cover with cling film in direct contact and leave to cool in the fridge.

FOR THE CARAMELISED PUFFED RICE

40 g caster sugar
15 g still mineral water
30 g puffed rice

Heat the sugar and water together in a saucepan until a thermometer or electronic probe reads 118°C. Pour over the puffed rice (previously heated) and mix, then leave to caramelise. Spread out over a baking tray covered with a non-stick silicone mat and leave to cool.

FOR THE PUFFED HAZELNUT PRALINE

18 g almond milk chocolate (Amatika 46% Valrhona® cocoa)
6 g deodorised coconut oil or margarine
15 g hazelnut praline (60-65% hazelnuts)
45 g pure roasted hazelnut paste (100% hazelnuts)
21 g caramelised puffed rice
21 g crushed roasted Piedmont hazelnuts

Melt the chocolate and margarine at 45°C in a bain-marie. Mix the hazelnut praline and the pure hazelnut paste and add to the previous mixture. Add the lightly chopped caramelised puffed rice and the crushed roasted Piedmont hazelnuts. On a stainless steel baking tray covered with greaseproof paper, spread the hazelnut puffed praline to a thickness of 1 cm and leave to set in the fridge. Cut into 1 cm squares. Freeze and store in an airtight container in the freezer.

FOR THE LEMON GEL

15 g caster sugar
1.7 g agar-agar powder
85 g organic lemon juice

In a mixing bowl, combine the sugar and agar-agar powder. In a saucepan, heat the lemon juice to 40°C, then sprinkle in the sugar/agar-agar mixture. Bring the mixture to the boil, stirring regularly. Remove from the heat and leave to cool completely in the fridge. Before use, blend the mixture in a food processor to transform it into a smooth, supple gel.

Note: this gel cannot be frozen.

FOR THE HAZELNUT CRUMBLE
36 g deodorised coconut oil
48 g ground hazelnuts
1 g Guérande fleur de sel
36 g caster sugar
46 g T45 fine wheat flour
13 g still mineral water
17.5 g crushed roasted hazelnuts

Melt the deodorised coconut oil at 30–35°C. Add the ground hazelnut powder, fleur de sel, sugar and flour to the bowl of a food processor fitted with a flat beater attachment, then add the coconut oil, at 30°C. Mix until well incorporated, then add the water (heated to 40°C) and the crushed roasted hazelnuts. Transfer to a baking tray and refrigerate for 2 hours. Press the mixture through a very large-holed sieve. Spread the crumble out on a baking tray lined with greaseproof paper taking care that it doesn't overlap. Bake in a fan oven at 160°C for around 20 minutes until golden brown.

FOR THE HAZELNUT TUILE
42 g deodorised coconut oil
60 g inverted sugar
40 g caster sugar
50 g plain flour
8 g still mineral water

Melt the deodorised coconut oil at 30–35°C. In the bowl of a food processor fitted with a flat beater attachment, mix the ingredients in order and leave to stand for 30 minutes at room temperature. Use immediately.

On a baking tray covered with a non-stick silicone mat, place a *mashrabiya* (Moorish-style) silicone mould, 5–6 cm in diameter, with cavities and spread the tuile dough evenly. Bake in a fan oven at 160°C for around 5 minutes. Turn over on the non-stick silicone mat and carefully remove from the mould. Leave to cool and use immediately or store in an airtight container.

Note: the tuiles will keep for several days.

(Cont.)

FOR THE CRUSHED CARAMELISED HAZELNUTS

125 g caster sugar
40 g still mineral water
300 g chopped roasted Piedmont hazelnuts
5 g cocoa butter (Valrhona®)

In a saucepan, heat the water and sugar to 118°C, checking using a thermometer or electronic probe, and pour over the hot roasted Piedmont hazelnuts. Mix and leave to caramelise. Once the hazelnuts are caramelised, add the cocoa butter and pour onto a baking tray covered with a non-stick silicone mat, spreading out as much as possible to cool. Crush them coarsely and use immediately.

Note: for the caramelised hazelnuts, wait until they have cooled before crushing them.

ASSEMBLY

Whip the lemon cream in the bowl of a food processor fitted with a whisk attachment, then set aside in the fridge for 1 hour. Place the disc of hazelnut leonard biscuit in the base of the dish, then, using a piping bag fitted with a plain No. 9 tip, pipe a spiral of smooth hazelnut cream over the entire disc. Lightly press cubes of homemade semi-confit lemon and cubes of puffed hazelnut praline into the cream. Using a piping bag without a tip, pipe balls of lemon gel. Pipe the whipped lemon cream. Refrigerate for 1 hour. Just before serving, sprinkle pieces of hazelnut crumble and crushed caramelised hazelnuts over the cream, and top with lemon segments and semi-confit lemon strips. Top with 3 hazelnut tuiles and serve immediately.

Floating islands

Fomico mousse is generally made with fruit. In this version, I've used oat and soya milks to prepare the quenelles that are placed on top of the custard.

Linda Vongdara

Serves 6

Preparation time: 2 hours
Resting time: 4 hours
Cooking time: 15 minutes

FOR THE VEGAN MILK FOMICO MOUSSE

100 g liquid yumgo white (or 160 g aquafaba)
40 g light brown sugar
200 g plain soya milk
200 g oat milk
2 g agar-agar powder

In the bowl of a food processor fitted with a whisk attachment, blend the yumgo white and gradually add the sugar until it forms stiff peaks. Remove the bowl from the food processor. Bring the 2 milks and the agar-agar to the boil. Off the heat, add a third of the mousse from the yumgo and sugar mixture to the saucepan and whisk to combine. Then pour the mixture from the saucepan into the bowl of the food processor and finish whisking from top to bottom. Form 18 quenelles (3 per dessert) using a lightly oiled tablespoon and leave to cool on a tray covered with cling film.

FOR THE VEGAN CUSTARD

3 Tahiti vanilla pods
400 g almond milk
400 g oat milk
80 g light brown sugar
15 g cornflour
50 g cashew nut butter

Split and scrape the vanilla pods. In a saucepan, mix the 2 milks, the sugar, vanilla and cornflour. Bring to the boil. Remove from the heat, add the cashew nut butter and blend using an immersion blender. Leave to cool and set aside in the fridge until ready to use.

FOR THE ROASTED ALMONDS
100 g flaked almonds
50 g caster sugar
5 g deodorised coconut oil

In a frying pan, heat all the ingredients over a high heat until the sugar has caramelised. Transfer the almonds onto a sheet of greaseproof paper and let cool.

FOR THE ANGEL HAIR
300 g caster sugar
100 g still mineral water

Protect the work surface with a sheet of greaseproof paper. Place 2 metal rods or bars parallel to each other, spaced about 15 cm apart. Use a support at each end of the rods so that they do not touch the worktop. In a saucepan, heat the sugar and water to the spun sugar stage, around 165-170°C, checking using a thermometer or electronic probe. To stop the caramel cooking, place the bottom of the pan in a bowl of cold water. Dip a whisk into the caramel and swing it over the rods. Threads will form between the two. Repeat as many times as necessary. Collect the angel hair that has solidified to shape it. Use immediately.

ASSEMBLY

Pour the custard into the dishes and top with 3 quenelles of fomico mousse. Just before serving, sprinkle with the roasted almonds and top with the angel hair.

Note: the caramel must be golden brown to express its full flavour.

PLATED DESSERTS *Desserts to share... or not*

Floating islands with mango and coconut milk rice

Inspired by a recipe widely used in Laos, where my parents come from, this floating island combines the flavours of mango with glutinous rice cooked in coconut milk with a hint of fleur de sel.

Linda Vongdara

Serves 6

Preparation time: 4 hours
Resting time: 6 hours
Cooking time: 30 minutes

FOR THE MANGO MOUSSE DOME
50 g liquid yumgo white (or 80 g aquafaba)
25 g light brown sugar
200 g mango purée
1 g agar-agar powder

In the bowl of a food processor fitted with a whisk attachment, blend the yumgo white and gradually add the sugar until it forms stiff peaks. Remove the bowl from the food processor. Bring the mango purée and agar-agar to the boil. Off the heat, add a third of the yumgo and sugar mixture to the saucepan and whisk to combine. Then pour the mixture from the saucepan into the bowl of the food processor and finish whisking from top to bottom. Pour the mousse into 6 half-sphere silicone moulds, 6 cm diameter half-sphere. Leave to cool and set aside in the fridge until ready to use.

FOR THE PLAIN MOUSSE
50 g liquid yumgo white
40 g light brown sugar
200 g plain soya milk
1 g agar-agar powder

In the bowl of a food processor fitted with a whisk attachment, blend the yumgo white and gradually add the sugar until you it forms stiff peaks. Remove the bowl from the food processor. Bring the soya milk and agar-agar to the boil. Off the heat, add a third the yumgo and sugar mixture to the saucepan and whisk to combine. Then pour the mixture from the saucepan into the bowl of the food processor and finish whisking from top to bottom. Pour the mousse into a 20 cm square stainless steel frame and smooth. Leave to cool in the fridge and cut into 2 cm cubes.

FOR THE COCONUT MILK RICE SAUCE
600 g coconut milk
300 g oat milk
45 g Thai rice flour
90 g light brown sugar
1.5 g Guérande fleur de sel

Mix the ingredients in a saucepan and bring to the boil. Allow to cool and then store in the fridge.

FOR THE ASSEMBLY
Shredded coconut
Fresh coconut shavings (½ coconut)
Fresh mango balls (1 whole mango)
Zest of 1 lime

Pour the chilled coconut rice sauce into the bottom of the dishes. Unmould the mango mousse domes and carefully place 1 dome on top of the sauce, then sprinkle the domed side with grated coconut. Decorate with fresh mango balls, plain fomico mousse cubes or balls, fresh coconut shavings and lime zest.

Note: to use aquafaba instead of yumgo white, you need 80 g of aquafaba to replace the 50 g of yumgo. We recommend boiling the aquafaba with the sugar to thicken it and make it syrupy. Then simply whisk the mixture while still warm.

Vanilla and caramel brioche French toast

In this infinitely indulgent dessert, I needed to rediscover the moist, warm, caramelised flavour that I love so much in French toast. We succeeded in finding the right balance between coconut oil and non-dairy cream to replace the butter. This brioche French toast goes deliciously well with a scoop of Infinitely hazelnut or vanilla ice cream, or perhaps even the coconut.

Pierre Hermé

Makes 8 brioche French toasts

Preparation time: 6 hours
Resting time: 15 hours
Cooking time: 1 hour

FOR THE HYDRATED SEED MIX (PREPARE THE DAY BEFORE)
10 g chia seeds
10 g flaxseed
10 g rolled oats
30 g still mineral water

Using a food processor, coarsely blend the seeds and oats 30 minutes before preparing the brioche dough, to allow the seeds to hydrate. Add the water at room temperature.

PLATED DESSERTS *Desserts to share... or not*

FOR THE BRIOCHE DOUGH (PREPARE THE DAY BEFORE)

107.5 g cocoa butter (Valrhona®)
107.5 g deodorised coconut oil
425 g T45 flour
65 g caster sugar
20 g fresh yeast
6 g sunflower lecithin
310 g still mineral water
10 g Guérande fleur de sel
60 g hydrated seed mix

Melt the deodorised coconut oil and cocoa butter, then keep the mixture at 25°C. Place the sifted flour, sugar, fresh yeast and sunflower lecithin in the bowl of a food processor fitted with a dough hook or a flat beater attachment for small quantities. Run the processor on speed 1 and add around 70% of the still mineral water. Let the dough rise on speed 1 and add the remaining water in two batches, allowing it to rise between each addition. As soon as the dough comes away from the sides of the bowl, add the fleur de sel, the hydrated seeds and the mixture of cocoa butter and deodorised coconut oil at 25°C. Run the processor on speed 2 and wait for the dough to come away from the sides of the bowl. Transfer to a mixing bowl, cover with cling film in direct contact and leave to rise for 1 hour at room temperature. Fold the dough over slightly and set aside in the fridge. Leave to rise for 2 hours to 2 hours 30 minutes. Fold the dough over again and set aside in the fridge for about 12 hours. As soon as the dough is uniformly cold it is ready to be worked and rolled out.

FOR THE SHAPING AND COOKING

1 kg brioche dough
Margarine (as needed)

Lightly grease 4 cake moulds measuring 14 x 8 cm and 8 cm high. Shape the dough into 4 balls weighing 250 g each and place them in the moulds, pressing lightly. Leave to stand in a room at 28°C for 3 hours. Bake in a fan oven at 160°C for around 45-55 minutes, opening the oven door for a few seconds every 10 minutes to let the moisture escape. Allow to cool before turning out.

FOR THE EGGNOG MIXTURE

1 kg oat milk
100 g caster sugar
35 g cornflour
1.25 g natural orange flower flavouring

Mix together the sugar and cornflour. Mix with the oat milk and bring to the boil. Add the natural orange flower flavouring. Blend and use immediately or keep refrigerated.

FOR THE VANILLA CARAMEL

95 g oat milk
95 g non-dairy cream
1 Madagascar vanilla pod
70 g deodorised coconut oil or margarine
150 g caster sugar
1.5 g Guérande fleur de sel
0.4 g xanthan gum

Bring the oat milk and vegetable cream to the boil in a saucepan. Add the split and scraped vanilla pod and leave to infuse for 30 minutes. In another saucepan, make a dry caramel by gradually adding the sugar while stirring with a wooden spatula. When the caramel has a nice amber colour, gradually add the oat milk/non-dairy cream mixture, then the deodorised coconut oil. Bring to the boil. Using an immersion blender, blend in the xanthan gum and fleur de sel. Keep refrigerated in an airtight container covered with cling film in direct contact.

FOR THE VANILLA ICE CREAM

410 g oat milk
3 Madagascar vanilla pods
20 g inulin
75 g caster sugar
40 g inverted sugar
60 g deodorised coconut oil
0.75 g guar gum
0.75 g carob bean gum
1.5 g citrus fibre

Pour the oat milk into a saucepan and bring to the boil. Add the split and scraped vanilla pods, leave to infuse for 30 minutes and strain. Pour the vanilla-infused oat milk into a saucepan and heat. At 25°C, add the inulin. At 30°C, add 70 g of the sugar and the inverted sugar. At 40°C, add the deodorised coconut oil, previously melted at 40°C. At 45°C, add the guar gum, carob bean gum and citrus fibre plus the remaining sugar. Cook the mixture at 85°C, checking using a thermometer or electronic probe, for 2 minutes. Using an immersion blender, blend the mixture and leave to cool to 4°C. Leave to stand for at least 4 hours in the fridge before churning. Place a stainless steel tray in the freezer for 30 minutes. Using an immersion blender, blend the ice cream a second time. Churn the vanilla ice cream. Once out of the ice-cream maker, pour the ice cream into the stainless steel tray and set aside in the freezer.

FOR CUTTING AND BAKING THE BRIOCHE FRENCH TOAST

600 g caster sugar
50 g margarine

Using a ruler, cut 2.5 cm thick slices of brioche with the crust. Pour the eggnog mixture into a tin and place the slices of brioche on top. Refrigerate for at least 1 hour. When serving, before caramelising the brioche, drain it to remove any excess eggnog. In a frying pan, make a dry caramel with the sugar, then deglaze with the margarine. Once you have made the caramel, use it to coat both sides of the brioche slices. If the caramel doesn't stick to the brioche, dilute it with a little eggnog. Place the French toast on a plate, top with a scoop of vanilla ice cream and drizzle with vanilla caramel.

Note: the brioche French toast can also be caramelised in advance and baked in the oven just before serving.

PLATED DESSERTS *Desserts to share... or not*

An introduction to the tastes, textures and temperatures of pure origin Ecuador chocolate

I imagined this dessert as a journey through the world of chocolate. I like the idea of giving diners the freedom to experience each bite differently.

Pierre Hermé

Serves 10

Preparation time: 6 hours
Resting time: 12 hours
Cooking time: 30 minutes

FOR THE HACIENDA ELEONOR SMOOTH CHOCOLATE CREAM (PREPARE THE DAY BEFORE)

130 g dark chocolate (Hacienda Eleonor Pure Origin Ecuador 64% Valrhona® cocoa)
50 g caster sugar
5 g pectin X58
275 g oat milk
0.5 g Guérande fleur de sel
25 g deodorised coconut oil
15 g sunflower oil

Chop the dark chocolate. Mix together the sugar and pectin. In a saucepan, heat the oat milk to 40°C, checking using a thermometer or electronic probe, and add the fleur de sel and sugar/pectin mixture. Bring to the boil, then pour over the chopped chocolate and oils in three batches. Blend and set aside in a casserole dish, covered with cling film in direct contact. Refrigerate for 12 hours before use.

FOR THE HACIENDA ELEONOR CHOCOLATE CHANTILLY CREAM (PREPARE THE DAY BEFORE)

335 g oat milk
200 g dark chocolate (Hacienda Eleonor pure origin Ecuador 64% Valrhona® cocoa)

Chop the chocolate. Bring the oat milk to the boil, then pour over the chopped chocolate. Stir starting from the centre and working outwards. Using an immersion blender, blend the cream. Place in a casserole dish, cover with cling film in direct contact and leave to cool and set in the fridge for around 12 hours. This cream can be frozen as it is.

FOR THE HACIENDA ELEONOR CHOCOLATE SHARDS WITH FLEUR DE SEL

200 g dark chocolate (Hacienda Eleonor pure origin Ecuador 64% Valrhona® cocoa)
3.6 g Guérande fleur de sel

Finely crush the fleur de sel crystals with a rolling pin, then sieve through a medium/fine sieve. Set aside the finest crystals. Temper the dark chocolate to keep it shiny, smooth and stable. Chop the chocolate with a serrated knife and place in an earthenware bowl, then melt it in a bain-marie. Stir gently with a wooden spoon until it reaches 50-55°C. Remove the chocolate from the bain-marie. Place the bowl in a second bowl filled with water and 4-5 ice cubes. Stir the melted chocolate from time to time as it will start to set on the sides of the bowl. As soon as it reaches 27-28°C, return the bowl to the bain-marie, keeping a close eye on the temperature. When it reaches 31-32°C, the chocolate is tempered. Stir in the fleur de sel. On a plastic sheet, thinly spread the tempered fleur de sel chocolate to a thickness of about 1 cm. Cover with a second plastic sheet and a weight on top to prevent the chocolate from warping as it sets. Refrigerate for a few hours. Coarsely break the fleur de sel chocolate slabs into 5-7 cm shards for decoration. Keep in an airtight container in the fridge.

FOR THE HACIENDA ELEONOR CHOCOLATE SORBET

355 g still mineral water
55 g caster sugar
2 g guar gum
2 g carob bean gum
16.5 g cocoa powder
35 g dark chocolate (Hacienda Eleonor pure origin Ecuador 64% Valrhona® cocoa)

Pour the water into a saucepan and heat. At 30°C, add 90% of the sugar. At 45°C, add the guar gum and carob bean gum with the remaining 10% of the sugar. Pour 250 g of the liquid (two thirds of the weight of chocolate) over the melted chocolate and cocoa powder, stirring in the centre to create an elastic, shiny core, the sign that the emulsion has begun. Gradually add the remaining liquid. Blend with an immersion blender to emulsify. Bring everything together in the saucepan and cook at

85°C (checking using a thermometer or electronic probe) for 2 minutes, then cool rapidly to 4°C. Pour into the ice-cream maker and churn. Remove and set aside in the freezer.

FOR THE INFINITELY CHOCOLATE SHORTBREAD

75 g margarine
60 g light brown sugar
25 g caster sugar
2.5 g Guérande fleur de sel
1 g natural vanilla extract
75 g dark chocolate (Araguani 72% Valrhona® cocoa)
90 g plain flour
15 g cocoa powder (Valrhona®)
2.5 g baking soda

Using a food processor, blend the chocolate into small pieces. Sift in the flour, cocoa powder and baking soda. In the bowl of a food processor fitted with a flat beater attachment, cream the margarine, then add the sugars, fleur de sel and natural vanilla extract, followed by the flour/cocoa powder/baking soda mixture and the blended chocolate. Mix as little as possible, as with shortbread, and use immediately. On a lightly floured work surface, roll out the infinitely chocolate shortbread dough to a thickness of about 7 mm. Leave to cool, then cut into 7 mm cubes. Cover with cling film and set aside in the fridge. Place the cubes 1.5 cm apart on a baking tray lined with greaseproof paper. Bake in a fan oven at 165°C for 10 minutes. Leave to cool, then use immediately or store in an airtight container at room temperature.

FOR THE NOUGATINE WITH COCOA NIBS

20 g still mineral water
20 g glucose syrup
60 g caster sugar
1 g pectin NH
26 g rapeseed or grapeseed oil
1 g citrus fibre
60 g cocoa nibs (Valrhona®)
0.4 g Sarawak black pepper

In a saucepan, heat the water and glucose syrup to 45-50°C. Add a mixture of the sugar and pectin and heat to 106°C, checking using a thermometer or electronic probe. Add the oil and citrus fibre and blend using an immersion blender. Add the cocoa nibs and ground black pepper. Pour the mixture onto a sheet of greaseproof paper and spread with a palette knife. Cover with another sheet of greaseproof paper and continue to spread by pressing with a rolling pin over the sheets. Freeze and keep wrapped in cling film in the freezer.

FOR FINISHING

Guérande fleur de sel (as needed)
Sarawak black pepper (as needed)

FINISHING AND COOKING

Place the raw nougatine on a baking tray lined with greaseproof paper. Sprinkle evenly with a pinch of fleur de sel and add 2 turns of Sarawak black pepper. Cook in a fan oven at 170°C for 18-20 minutes. Leave to cool and use immediately or store in an airtight container at room temperature.

(Cont.)

FOR THE HACIENDA ELEONOR COLD CHOCOLATE SAUCE

300 g still mineral water
10 g caster sugar
0.5 g Guérande fleur de sel
160 g dark chocolate (Hacienda Eleonor pure origin Ecuador 64% Valrhona® cocoa)

Bring the water to the boil in a saucepan, then dissolve the sugar and fleur de sel in it. Pour over the chopped chocolate in three batches, stirring after each addition. Blend with an immersion blender and refrigerate. Whisk before use.

ASSEMBLY

Whip the chocolate chantilly cream in the bowl of a food processor fitted with a flat beater attachment and use immediately. On the centre line of an oval plate, crumble 3 cubes of Infinitely chocolate shortbread and place the quenelles on top. Add a quenelle of chocolate sorbet, a quenelle of chocolate chantilly and a quenelle of smooth chocolate cream. Place cubes of Infinitely chocolate shortbread on top. Add the chocolate shards with fleur de sel and nougatine with cocoa nibs on the quenelles. Prepare a sauce boat of cold chocolate sauce. Enjoy immediately.

Ouréa dessert

The combination of Ouréa flavours lends itself to multiple interpretations. The bright flavours of the sorbet and the yuzu purée come to the fore first, highlighting the sweet, gourmet notes of the Piedmont hazelnut in a fresh, tangy and infinitely delicious ripple.

Pierre Hermé

Makes 10 desserts

Preparation time: 6 hours
Resting time: 17 hours
Cooking time: 30 minutes

FOR THE SMOOTH HAZELNUT CREAM (PREPARE THE DAY BEFORE)

500 g still mineral water
125 g glucose syrup
100 g cocoa butter (Valrhona®)
650 g pure roasted hazelnut paste (100% hazelnuts)
350 g hazelnut praline (60-65% hazelnuts)

Pour the water and glucose syrup into a saucepan and bring to the boil. Immediately pour over the chopped cocoa butter, the pure hazelnut paste and the hazelnut praline in 2 batches mixing after each addition. Using an immersion blender, blend to a smooth cream. Place in a casserole dish, cover with cling film in direct contact and leave to cool. Refrigerate for 12 hours before use.

FOR THE HOMEMADE KÔCHI YUZU PURÉE

5 g caster sugar
5 g pectin NH
65 g Kôchi yuzu juice
125 g candied yuzu peel
25 g still mineral water

Mix together the sugar and pectin. Using a food processor, blend the juice and candied yuzu peel into small pieces. Heat the water and the yuzu peel/juice mixture in a saucepan, checking the temperature using a thermometer or electronic probe. When the mixture reaches 40°C, sprinkle in the sugar and pectin. Bring to the boil. Set aside in the fridge.

FOR THE CARAMELISED PUFFED RICE

200 g caster sugar
75 g still mineral water
150 g puffed rice
1 g fleur de sel

Heat the sugar and water together in a saucepan until a thermometer or electronic probe reads 118°C. Pour over the puffed rice (previously heated in the oven to 150°C for 5 minutes) and mix, stirring gently, then leave to caramelise over a medium heat. Add the fleur de sel. Transfer to a non-stick silicone mat to cool.

FOR THE CRUSHED ROASTED PIEDMONT HAZELNUTS

150 g unpeeled Piedmont hazelnuts

On a baking tray lined with greaseproof paper, spread out the hazelnuts, taking care that they don't overlap. Roast them in a fan oven at 165°C for 15 minutes. Remove the skin by passing them through a large-mesh sieve. Using a knife, on a chopping board, coarsely crush them. Use immediately or store in an airtight container at room temperature.

FOR THE PUFFED HAZELNUT PRALINE

75 g almond milk chocolate (Amatika 46% Valrhona® cocoa)
25 g deodorised coconut oil or margarine
60 g hazelnut praline (60-65% hazelnuts)
180 g pure roasted hazelnut paste (100% hazelnuts)
85 g caramelised puffed rice
85 g crushed roasted Piedmont hazelnuts

Melt the chocolate and fat in a bain-marie at 45°C, checking using a thermometer or electronic probe. Mix the hazelnut praline and the pure hazelnut paste and add to the previous mixture. Add the lightly chopped caramelised puffed rice and the crushed roasted Piedmont hazelnuts. On a stainless steel baking tray covered with greaseproof paper, spread the hazelnut puffed praline to a thickness of 1 cm and leave to set in the fridge. Using a knife and a chopping board, cut into 1 cm cubes. Cover with cling film and freeze.

FOR THE HAZELNUT CRUMBLE

72 g deodorised coconut oil
96 g ground hazelnuts
2 g Guérande fleur de sel
72 g caster sugar
92 g flour
26 g still mineral water
35 g crushed roasted Piedmont hazelnuts

Melt the coconut oil at 30-35°C, checking using a thermometer or electronic probe. Place the ground hazelnuts, fleur de sel, sugar and sifted flour in the bowl of a food processor fitted with a flat beater attachment, then pour in the coconut oil, melted at 30°C. Blend until well incorporated, then add the water (heated to 40°C) and the crushed roasted hazelnuts. Place on a baking tray lined with greaseproof paper and refrigerate for 2 hours. Press the mixture through a very large-holed sieve. Spread the crumble out on a baking tray lined with greaseproof paper taking care that it doesn't overlap. Bake in a fan oven at 160°C for around 20 minutes until golden brown. Allow to cool and then store in a dry place.

FOR THE YUZU SORBET

5 g organic lemon zest
210 g caster sugar
405 g still mineral water
2.5 g dried yuzu powder
70 g atomised glucose
17.5 g inulin
1.5 g guar gum
1.5 g carob bean gum
285 g Kôchi yuzu juice

Using a Microplane® grater, remove the lemon zest and mix with half of the sugar. In a saucepan, heat the water and sugar mixed with the zest, yuzu powder, atomised glucose and inulin. At 45°C, add the guar gum and carob bean gum mixed with the remaining sugar. Cook the mixture at 85°C, checking using a thermometer or electronic probe, for 2 minutes. Using an immersion blender, blend the mixture and leave to cool to 4°C. Leave to stand for at least 4 hours before churning. Add the yuzu juice, blend again and churn. Set aside in the freezer.

FOR THE CRISPY TUILE

84 g deodorised coconut oil
120 g inverted sugar
80 g caster sugar
100 g flour
16 g still mineral water

Melt the deodorised coconut oil at 30-35°C, checking using a thermometer or electronic probe, then add the ingredients in order and mix. Leave at room temperature for 30 minutes. On a baking tray lined with a non-stick silicone mat, place a leaf-shaped cavity silicone mould and spread the tuile mixture evenly. Bake in a fan oven at 160°C for around 5 minutes. Turn the mould over on the mat and carefully unmould. Store in an airtight container away from moisture. The tuiles will keep for several days.

FOR THE ASSEMBLY

Candied yuzu peel (as needed)

Using a piping bag fitted with a No. 12 plain tip, pipe a 30 g spiral of smooth hazelnut cream onto the centre of a plate. Using a piping bag without a tip, pipe dots of Kôchi yuzu purée, add cubes of puffed hazelnut praline, pieces of hazelnut crumble and candied yuzu peel. In the middle, place a scoop of yuzu sorbet and on top, slightly offset, add a tuile. Enjoy immediately.

Almond and vanilla millefeuille

One of the great classics of French pastry-making, the millefeuille needed a vegan version. Here it is served with an almond and vanilla cream to keep the flavours simple and straightforward.

Linda Vongdara

Makes 11 individual millefeuilles

Preparation time: 6 hours
Resting time: 6 hours
Cooking time: 45 minutes

FOR THE INVERTED PUFF PASTRY
1) MARGARINE/FLOUR
375 g pastry margarine
150 g T45 flour

In the bowl of a food processor fitted with a flat beater attachment, cream the margarine. Add the sifted flour and mix as little as possible until the mixture is smooth. Roll out in a rectangle on a sheet of greaseproof paper, cover with a second sheet of greaseproof paper and refrigerate for 1 hour.

2) DÉTREMPE (PUFF PASTRY DOUGH)
115 g pastry margarine
150 g still mineral water
2.5 g white vinegar
17.5 g Guérande fleur de sel
350 g T45 flour

Soften the margarine in the microwave. Mix all the ingredients in the bowl of a food processor fitted with a dough hook. Roll out the dough into a square on a baking tray lined with greaseproof paper, cover with cling film and leave in the fridge for 1 hour.

Wrap the détrempe round the margarine/flour mixture. The two elements should have an identical texture. Roll out the pastry lengthways and make two double turns at 2-hour intervals, leaving the pastry to rest in the fridge between each turn. Then make a simple turn before cutting. Puff pastry with two double turns can be kept for several days in the fridge.

ROLLING OUT THE INVERTED PUFF PASTRY

On a lightly floured work surface, roll out the puff pastry to a thickness of around 2 mm, prick it with a fork and then cut it to the size of a baking tray. Place a sheet of greaseproof paper on the baking tray and add the pastry on top. Place the baking tray in the fridge: the dough needs to rest for at least 2 hours to develop properly in the oven and cook without shrinking. You can keep the puff pastry in the freezer.

FOR THE CARAMELISED INVERTED PUFF PASTRY
80 g caster sugar
50 g icing sugar

Place the inverted puff pastry on a baking tray lined with greaseproof paper. Sprinkle the pastry evenly with 80 g (for a 60 x 40 cm sheet) of caster sugar and place in a fan oven at 230°C. Immediately lower the temperature to 190°C and cook the pastry for 10 minutes, then cover it with a stainless steel wire rack to prevent it from rising too much and continue cooking for a further 10 minutes. Add a baking tray to the wire rack, pressing down gently, and continue cooking for a further 10 minutes. Remove the pastry from the oven, remove the baking tray and the rack, cover the pastry with a sheet of greaseproof paper and then a second baking tray, identical to the first. Turn the two baking sheets upside down, holding them together. On a work surface, remove the top baking tray and the sheet of greaseproof paper used for the first stage of cooking. Sprinkle the pastry evenly with icing sugar before placing it in the oven at 250°C to finish baking. During the final few minutes of cooking, the icing sugar will turn yellow before melting and caramelising. Remove the pastry from the oven: the surface should be smooth and shiny and the underside matt and crisp. Leave to cool. Along the width of the sheet of caramelised inverted puff pastry, cut 3 strips 11 cm wide and set aside for the assembly.

Note: never overcook the caramelised puff pastry, as this will give the cake a bitter taste.

FOR THE CREAMY ALMOND AND VANILLA CRÉMEUX

500 g vanilla soya milk
80 g cornflour
6 g agar-agar powder
290 g light brown sugar
220 g roasted almond butter
3 g Guérande fleur de sel
200 g deodorised coconut oil

In a saucepan, bring the soya milk, cornflour, agar-agar and light brown sugar to the boil. Using an immersion blender, emulsify the hot mixture with the almond butter, fleur de sel and deodorised coconut oil. Chill quickly in the fridge until ready to use.

FOR THE CARAMELISED ALMONDS

70 g white almonds
250 g caster sugar
75 g still mineral water

On a baking tray lined with greaseproof paper, spread out the almonds taking care that they don't overlap. Roast them in a fan oven at 165°C for 15 minutes. In a saucepan, heat the water and sugar to 118°C, checking using a thermometer or electronic probe, then add the warm almonds. Caramelise over a low heat. Pour the caramelised almonds onto a baking tray lined with a non-stick silicone mat, then separate them to cool. Store in an airtight container.

ASSEMBLY

On a baking tray, lay a first strip of caramelised inverted puff pastry, shiny caramelised side up. Using a piping bag fitted with a No. 14 plain tip, pipe half the almond and vanilla crémeux. Place the second strip of caramelised inverted puff pastry on top, then top with the remaining crémeux. Finish with the third strip of caramelised inverted puff pastry and press lightly. Leave to set in the fridge and cut into 11 even millefeuilles. Proceed with the finishing.

FOR FINISHING

Place a caramelised almond on each millefeuille. Keep in the fridge until ready to use.

2000 feuilles

The vegan interpretation of this 2000 feuilles had to be a bite of pure pleasure. The strong flavour of the hazelnut praline and the crispness of the puff pastry make you forget that there's no butter, creating a tasting experience of 2000 sensations.

Pierre Hermé

Makes 11 individual 2000 feuilles

Preparation time: 6 hours
Resting time: 6 hours
Cooking time: 45 minutes

FOR THE INVERTED PUFF PASTRY
1) MARGARINE/FLOUR
375 g pastry margarine
150 g T45 flour

In the bowl of a food processor fitted with a flat beater attachment, cream the margarine. Add the sifted flour and mix as little as possible until the mixture is smooth. Roll out in a rectangle on a sheet of greaseproof paper, cover with a second sheet of greaseproof paper and refrigerate for 1 hour.

2) DÉTREMPE (PUFF PASTRY DOUGH)
115 g pastry margarine
150 g still mineral water
2.5 g white vinegar
17.5 g Guérande fleur de sel
350 g T45 flour

Soften the pastry margarine in the microwave. Mix all the ingredients in the bowl of a food processor fitted with a dough hook. Roll out the dough into a square on a baking tray lined with greaseproof paper, cover with cling film and leave in the fridge for 1 hour. Wrap the détrempe round the margarine/flour mixture. The two elements should have an identical texture. Roll out the pastry lengthways and make two double turns at 2-hour intervals, leaving the pastry to rest in the fridge between each turn. Then make a simple turn before cutting. Puff pastry with two double turns can be kept for several days in the fridge.

ROLLING OUT THE INVERTED PUFF PASTRY

On a lightly floured work surface, roll out the puff pastry to a thickness of around 2 mm, prick it with a fork and then cut it to the size of a baking tray. Place a sheet of greaseproof paper on the baking tray and add the pastry on top. Place the baking tray in the fridge: the dough needs to rest for at least 2 hours to develop properly in the oven and cook without shrinking. You can keep the puff pastry in the freezer.

FOR THE CARAMELISED INVERTED PUFF PASTRY
80 g caster sugar
50 g icing sugar

Place the inverted puff pastry on a baking tray lined with greaseproof paper. Sprinkle the pastry evenly with 80 g (for a 60 x 40 cm sheet) of caster sugar and place in a fan oven at 230°C. Immediately lower the temperature to 190°C and cook the pastry for 10 minutes. Cover with a stainless steel wire rack to prevent it from rising too much and continue cooking for 10 minutes. Add a baking tray to the wire rack, pressing down gently, and continue cooking for a further 10 minutes. Remove the pastry from the oven, remove the baking tray and the rack, cover the pastry with a sheet of greaseproof paper and then a second baking tray, identical to the first. Turn the two baking sheets upside down, holding them together. On a work surface, remove the top baking tray and the sheet of greaseproof paper used for the first stage of cooking. Sprinkle the pastry evenly with icing sugar before placing it in the oven at 250°C to finish baking. During the final few minutes of cooking, the icing sugar will turn yellow before melting and caramelising. Remove the pastry from the oven: the surface should be smooth and shiny and the underside matt and crisp. Leave to cool. Along the width of the sheet of caramelised inverted puff pastry, cut 3 strips 11 cm wide and set aside for the assembly. For the finishing, set aside some flakes from the caramelised inverted puff pastry.

Note: never overcook the caramelised puff pastry, as this will give the cake a bitter taste.

FOR THE CRUSHED ROASTED PIEDMONT HAZELNUTS
100 g unpeeled Piedmont hazelnuts

On a baking tray lined with greaseproof paper, spread out the hazelnuts, taking care that they don't overlap. Roast them in a fan oven at 165°C for 15 minutes. Remove the skin by passing them through a large-mesh sieve. Using a knife, on a chopping board, coarsely crush them. Use immediately or store in an airtight container at room temperature.

FOR THE CARAMELISED PUFFED RICE
50 g caster sugar
20 g still mineral water
40 g puffed rice

Heat the sugar and water together in a saucepan until a thermometer or electronic probe reads 118°C. Pour in the puffed rice (previously heated) and mix, then leave to caramelise. Pour onto a baking tray covered with a non-stick silicone mat and leave to cool.

FOR THE PUFFED HAZELNUT PRALINE
75 g almond milk chocolate (Amatika 46% Valrhona® cocoa)
25 g deodorised coconut oil or margarine
60 g hazelnut praline (60-65% hazelnuts)
180 g pure roasted hazelnut paste (100% hazelnuts)
85 g caramelised puffed rice
85 g crushed roasted Piedmont hazelnuts

Melt the chocolate and fat in a bain-marie at 45°C. Mix the hazelnut praline and the pure hazelnut paste and add to the previous mixture. Add the lightly chopped caramelised puffed rice and the crushed roasted Piedmont hazelnuts. On a stainless steel baking tray covered with greaseproof paper, spread the hazelnut puffed praline over 25 x 22 cm and leave to set in the fridge. Using a knife and a cutting board, cut into 2 strips measuring 25 x 11 cm. Cover with cling film and freeze.

FOR THE PASTRY CREAM
16 g cornflour
135 g oat milk
26 g caster sugar
35 g margarine

Sift the cornflour. In a saucepan, bring the oat milk to the boil with a third of the caster sugar. Mix the cornflour and the remaining sugar. Mix this mixture with half the oat milk/sugar mixture before adding the other half. Bring the pastry cream to the boil, whisking briskly. Remove from the heat, add the margarine, stir and leave to cool. Set aside in the fridge.

FOR THE ITALIAN MERINGUE

150 g still mineral water
10 g pea protein
0.25 g xanthan gum
235 g caster sugar

Using an immersion blender, mix 105 g of the water, the pea protein and the xanthan gum together. Leave to rest for 20 minutes in the fridge before whipping the mixture at medium speed in the bowl of a food processor fitted with a whisk attachment. In a saucepan, heat the remaining water and sugar to 121°C, checking using a thermometer or electronic probe. Drizzle the sugar syrup over the water/protein/xanthan mixture. Leave to cool, blending at the same speed.

Note: once the meringue has cooled, it is best to let it run on low speed rather than letting it set, to improve the result and hold.

FOR THE PRALINE CREAM

345 cold Italian meringue (the recipe above once cooled)
375 g margarine
100 g hazelnut praline (60-65% hazelnuts)
80 g pure roasted hazelnut paste (100% hazelnuts)

In the bowl of a food processor fitted with a whisk attachment, cream the margarine at room temperature and add the Italian meringue by hand. Whisk to make a light and creamy mixture. When it is smooth and homogeneous, add the praline and the pure hazelnut paste. Mix and use immediately.

FOR THE PRALINE MOUSSELINE CREAM

175 g non-dairy cream (31% fat)
160 g pastry cream
835 g praline cream

Whip the non-dairy cream in the bowl of a food processor fitted with a whisk attachment. Using a whisk, smooth the pastry cream in a mixing bowl. In the bowl of a food processor fitted with a whisk attachment, whip the cold praline cream to make it light and creamy. When it is smooth and homogeneous, add the pastry cream. Gently fold in the whipped non-dairy cream with a spatula and use immediately.

FOR THE CARAMELISED PIEDMONT HAZELNUTS

70 g unpeeled Piedmont hazelnuts
250 g caster sugar
75 g still mineral water

On a baking tray lined with greaseproof paper, spread out the hazelnuts, taking care that they don't overlap. Roast them in a fan oven at 165°C for 15 minutes. Remove the skin by passing them through a large-mesh sieve. In a saucepan, heat the water and sugar to 118°C, checking using a thermometer or electronic probe, then add the warm hazelnuts. Caramelise over a low heat. Pour the caramelised hazelnuts onto a baking tray lined with a non-stick silicone mat then separate them to cool. Store in an airtight container.

FOR THE ASSEMBLY
Finely crushed caramelised inverted puff pastry flakes

On a baking tray, lay a first strip of caramelised inverted puff pastry, shiny caramelised side up. Using a piping bag fitted with a No. 14 plain tip, pipe 250 g of praline mousseline cream, place the strip of puffed hazelnut praline on top and pipe another 250 g of praline mousseline cream. Place the second strip of caramelised inverted puff pastry on top, then top with 500 g of praline mousseline cream. Finish with the third strip of caramelised inverted puff pastry, pressing down lightly and smoothing the cream over the edges. Add the finely crushed flakes of caramelised puff pastry, leave to set in the fridge and cut into approximately 11 even millefeuilles. Proceed with the finishing.

FOR FINISHING

Place a caramelised hazelnut on each 2000 feuille. Keep in the fridge until ready to use.

Note: inverted puff pastry has a number of advantages: it is both crispier and more melting, it shrinks less when cooked and keeps better when frozen.

Infinitely chocolate millefeuille

When there are no eggs or creams, the aromas of chocolate are expressed more purely. Combined with the crispness of the puff pastry, I rediscovered the emotions of an excellent millefeuille.

Pierre Hermé

Makes 11 individual millefeuilles

Preparation time: 6 hours
Resting time: 12 hours
Cooking time: 45 minutes

FOR THE DARK CHOCOLATE CHANTILLY CREAM (PREPARE THE DAY BEFORE)
670 g oat milk
400 g dark chocolate (Ampamakia 64% Valrhona® cocoa)

Chop the dark chocolate. Bring the oat milk to the boil in a saucepan, then pour over the chocolate. Stir starting from the centre and working outwards. Using an immersion blender, blend the mixture. Place in a casserole dish, cover with cling film in direct contact and leave to cool and set in the fridge for around 12 hours before use.

FOR THE INVERTED PUFF PASTRY
1) MARGARINE/FLOUR
375 g pastry margarine
150 g T45 flour

In the bowl of a food processor fitted with a flat beater attachment, cream the margarine. Add the sifted flour and mix as little as possible until the mixture is smooth. Roll out in a rectangle on a sheet of greaseproof paper, cover with a second sheet of greaseproof paper and refrigerate for 1 hour.

2) DÉTREMPE (PUFF PASTRY DOUGH)

115 g pastry margarine
150 g still mineral water
2.5 g white vinegar
17.5 g Guérande fleur de sel
350 g T45 flour

Soften the pastry margarine in the microwave. Mix all the ingredients in the bowl of a food processor fitted with a dough hook. Roll out the dough into a square on a baking tray lined with greaseproof paper, cover with cling film and leave in the fridge for 1 hour. Wrap the détrempe round the margarine/flour mixture. The two elements should have an identical texture. Roll out the pastry lengthways and make two double turns at 2-hour intervals, leaving the pastry to rest in the fridge between each turn. Then make a simple turn before cutting. Puff pastry with two double turns can be kept for several days in the fridge.

ROLLING OUT THE INVERTED PUFF PASTRY

On a lightly floured work surface, roll out the puff pastry to a thickness of around 2 mm, prick it with a fork and then cut it to the size of a baking tray. Place a sheet of greaseproof paper on the baking tray and add the pastry on top. Place the baking tray in the fridge: the dough needs to rest for at least 2 hours to develop properly in the oven and cook without shrinking. You can keep the puff pastry in the freezer.

FOR THE CARAMELISED INVERTED PUFF PASTRY

80 g caster sugar
50 g icing sugar

Place the inverted puff pastry on a baking tray lined with greaseproof paper. Sprinkle the pastry evenly with 80 g (for a 60 x 40 cm sheet) of caster sugar and place in a fan oven at 230°C. Immediately lower the temperature to 190°C and cook the pastry for 10 minutes, then cover it with a stainless steel wire rack to prevent it from rising too much and continue cooking for a further 10 minutes. Add a baking tray to the wire rack, pressing down gently, and continue cooking for a further 10 minutes. Remove the pastry from the oven, remove the baking tray and the rack, cover the pastry with a sheet of greaseproof paper and then a second baking tray, identical to the first. Turn the two baking sheets upside down, holding them together. On a work surface, remove the top baking tray and the sheet of greaseproof paper used for the first stage of cooking. Sprinkle the pastry evenly with icing sugar before placing it in the oven at 250°C to finish baking. During the final few minutes of cooking, the icing sugar will turn yellow before melting and caramelising. Remove the pastry from the oven: the surface should be smooth and shiny and the underside matt and crisp. Leave to cool. Along the width of the sheet of caramelised inverted puff pastry, cut 3 strips, 11 cm wide, then rectangles 2.5 cm wide. Set aside for assembly.

Note: never overcook the caramelised puff pastry, as this will give the cake a bitter taste.

FOR THE COCOA NIB CRUNCH
64 g deodorised coconut oil
144 g pure cocoa paste (100% Valrhona® cocoa)
576 g almond praline (60% almonds)
120 g cocoa nibs (Valrhona®)

In a large saucepan set over a bain-marie, melt the deodorised coconut oil and the pure cocoa paste at 45°C, checking using a thermometer or electronic probe. Mix in the almond praline and then the cocoa nibs.

Spread the cocoa nib crunch over a stainless steel baking tray covered with a plastic sheet. Refrigerate for 1 hour. Cut into rectangles measuring 11 x 2.5 cm. Set aside in the fridge or freezer.

FOR THE FLEUR DE SEL DARK CHOCOLATE SHARDS
500 g dark chocolate (64% Valrhona® cocoa)
9 g Guérande fleur de sel

Finely crush the fleur de sel crystals with a rolling pin, then sieve through a medium/fine sieve. Set aside the finest crystals.

Temper the dark chocolate to keep it shiny, smooth and stable. Chop the chocolate with a serrated knife and place in an earthenware bowl, then melt it in a bain-marie. Stir gently with a wooden spoon until it reaches 50–55°C. Remove the chocolate from the bain-marie. Place the bowl in a second bowl filled with water and 4–5 ice cubes. Stir the melted chocolate from time to time as it will start to set on the sides of the bowl. As soon as it reaches 27–28°C, return the bowl to the bain-marie, keeping a close eye on the temperature. When it reaches 31–32°C, the chocolate is tempered. Stir in the fleur de sel.

On a plastic sheet, spread the tempered fleur de sel chocolate to a thickness of about 1 mm. Cover with a second plastic sheet and a weight to prevent the chocolate from warping as it sets. Refrigerate for a few hours. Using a chopping board and a knife, roughly chop half the fleur de sel chocolate into 0.5 cm to 1 cm shards and set aside in an airtight container in the fridge for assembly. Use the other half of the fleur de sel chocolate to decorate the millefeuilles.

FOR THE ASSEMBLY

In the bowl of a food processor fitted with a whisk attachment, whip the dark chocolate chantilly. On a baking tray, place 10 rectangles of caramelised puff pastry, shiny caramelised side down. Using a piping bag fitted with a No. 12 plain tip, pipe balls of dark chocolate chantilly and sprinkle with fleur de sel dark chocolate shards. Place the second rectangle of caramelised puff pastry on top, caramelised side down, and pipe balls of dark chocolate chantilly. Finally, place the third rectangle of caramelised puff pastry on top, caramelised side up this time. Place the millefeuille on its side on a plate and sprinkle the entire surface with fleur de sel dark chocolate shards. Using a piping bag fitted with a No. 20 Saint Honoré tip, pipe the dark chocolate chantilly cream in a zigzag pattern over the entire surface of the millefeuille. Top with 3 large fleur de sel dark chocolate shards and serve immediately.

Note: inverted puff pastry has a number of advantages: it is both crispier and more melting, it shrinks less when cooked and keeps better when frozen.

Infinitely almond panna cotta

For me, this almond panna cotta is a shining example of clarity. It's a natural fit with the plant world. With a pure simplicity, the result is a perfect harmony of flavours and textures that brings out all the almond's characteristics. Amlou honey is a strong feature of this dessert, which is why it has been used in this recipe.

Pierre Hermé

Makes 10 desserts

Preparation time: 3 hours
Resting time: 6 hours
Cooking time: 45 minutes

FOR THE ROASTED ALMOND INFUSION
2.1 kg almond milk
840 g roasted unpeeled almonds

On a baking tray lined with greaseproof paper, spread out the almonds, taking care that they don't overlap. Roast them in a fan oven at 170°C for 15 minutes. Using a chopping board and a saucepan, coarsely crush the roasted almonds. Bring the almond milk and almonds to the boil in a saucepan, then using an immersion blender or food processor, blend as finely as possible. Cover and leave to infuse for 20 minutes before straining. Use immediately.

Note: you'll need the infusion for the cream and granita.

PLATED DESSERTS *Desserts to share... or not*

FOR THE ALMOND MILK PANNA COTTA CREAM

800 g roasted almond infusion
60 g caster sugar
200 g white almond butter
1.86 g iota carrageenan

Put the roasted almond infusion in a saucepan, add the sugar, almond butter and iota carrageenan and blend until smooth. Heat to 65°C, checking using a thermometer or electronic probe. Use immediately.

On a baking tray covered with a non-stick silicone mat, place 10 stainless steel rings 8 cm in diameter and 2 cm high, line them with a plastic strip and pour 85 g of panna cotta cream. Leave to cool in the fridge.

Note: this cream cannot be frozen! However the panna cotta cream discs can be kept for up to 3 days in the fridge.

FOR THE ALMOND GRANITA

150 g roasted almond infusion
400 g still mineral water
105 g caster sugar

Bring the ingredients to the boil and blend with an immersion blender. Pour into a stainless steel candissoire and leave to cool for 4 hours in the fridge. Freeze. Stir every 10 minutes to obtain large crystals. Once all the granita has been frozen, place in an airtight container and keep in the freezer.

FOR THE HOMEMADE AMLOU

400 g unpeeled almonds
0.5 g Guérande fleur de sel
40 g virgin argan oil
8 g orange or mixed-flower honey

On a baking tray lined with greaseproof paper, spread out the unpeeled almonds, taking care that they don't overlap. Roast them in a fan oven at 160°C for 35 minutes, then leave to cool. Using a food processor, grind the unpeeled almonds to a paste. Drizzle in the fleur de sel, honey and argan oil. Use immediately, or store in an airtight container in the fridge.

FOR THE CRUSHED CARAMELISED ALMONDS

300 g white almonds
40 g still mineral water
125 g caster sugar
5 g cocoa butter (Valrhona®)

On a baking tray lined with greaseproof paper, spread out the almonds, taking care that they don't overlap. Roast them in a fan oven at 170°C for 15 minutes. In a saucepan, heat the water and sugar to 118°C using a thermometer or electronic probe and pour in the warm almonds. Mix and leave to caramelise. Once the almonds are caramelised, add the cocoa butter and pour onto a stainless steel

baking tray covered with a non-stick silicone mat, spreading out as much as possible to cool. Crush them coarsely and use immediately.

Note: for the caramelised almonds, wait until they have cooled before crushing them.

FOR THE CARAMELISED FILO PASTRY
6 sheets filo pastry
Margarine (as needed)
Icing sugar (as needed)

Place a sheet of filo pastry on a sheet of greaseproof paper, brush with melted margarine, sprinkle with icing sugar and place a second sheet of filo pastry on top. Cut out 4 cm diameter discs. Repeat 3 times to obtain 100 discs of filo pastry.

Place the filo pastry discs on a baking tray lined with a non-stick silicone mat. Place a second non-stick silicone mat and a baking tray on top. Bake in a fan oven at 170°C for around 8 minutes. Leave to cool and store in an airtight container until ready to use.

Note: do not use too much margarine or too much sugar, as all the leaves will stick together when cooked and the pastry base will not be crisp.

ASSEMBLY

Using a piping bag pipe the amlou on to a very cold deep plate, taking care to centre it well. Place the almond milk panna cotta cream disc on top. Arrange the almond granita around the panna cotta. Place 10 discs of caramelised filo pastry on top of the cream. Place 3 caramelised almond halves in the centre and serve immediately.

Index by ingredient